UNION INTERNATIONALE DES SCIENCES PRÉHISTORIQUES ET PROTOHISTORIQUES
INTERNATIONAL UNION FOR PREHISTORIC AND PROTOHISTORIC SCIENCES

PROCEEDINGS OF THE XV WORLD CONGRESS (LISBON, 4-9 SEPTEMBER 2006)
ACTES DU XV CONGRÈS MONDIAL (LISBONNE, 4-9 SEPTEMBRE 2006)

Series Editor: Luiz Oosterbeek

VOL. 1

Session WC01

Status of Prehistoric Studies in the Twenty-First Century in India

État de l'art d'études préhistoriques au XXIe siècle en Inde

Edited by

Ranjana Ray
Vidula Jayaswal

BAR International Series 1924
2009

Published in 2016 by
BAR Publishing, Oxford

BAR International Series 1924

Proceedings of the XV World Congress of the International Union for Prehistoric and
Protohistoric Sciences /Actes du XV Congrès Mondial de l'Union Internationale des Sciences
Préhistoriques et Protohistoriques
Status of Prehistoric Studies in the Twenty-First Century in India /
État de l'art d'études préhistoriques au XXIe siècle en Inde

ISBN 978 1 4073 0406 9

Outgoing President: Vítor Oliveira Jorge; Outgoing Secretary General: Jean Bourgeois
Congress Secretary General: Luiz Oosterbeek (Series Editor)
Incoming President: Pedro Ignacio Shmitz
Incoming Secretary General: Luiz Oosterbeek
Volume Editors: Ranjana Ray and Vidula Jayaswal
Signed papers are the responsibility of their authors alone.
Les texts signés sont de la seule responsabilité de ses auteurs.
Contacts : Secretary of U.I.S.P.P. – International Union for Prehistoric and Protohistoric Sciences
Instituto Politécnico de Tomar, Av. Dr. Cândido Madureira 13, 2300 TOMAR
Email: uispp@ipt.pt   www.uispp.ipt.pt

BAR Publishing is the trading name of British Archaeological Reports (Oxford) Ltd.
British Archaeological Reports was first incorporated in 1974 to publish the BAR
Series, International and British. In 1992 Hadrian Books Ltd became part of the BAR
group. This volume was originally published by Archaeopress in conjunction with
British Archaeological Reports (Oxford) Ltd / Hadrian Books Ltd, the Series principal
publisher, in 2009. This present volume is published by BAR Publishing, 2016.

Printed in England

BAR
PUBLISHING

BAR titles are available from:

BAR Publishing
122 Banbury Rd, Oxford, OX2 7BP, UK
EMAIL   info@barpublishing.com
PHONE   +44 (0)1865 310431
FAX   +44 (0)1865 316916
www.barpublishing.com

TABLE OF CONTENTS

LIST OF FIGURES

LIST OF TABLES

STATUS OF PREHISTORIC STUDIES IN THE TWENTY FIRST CENTURY IN INDIA: AN INTRODUCTION

Ranjana RAY

Prehistoric research in India began in the nineteenth century, precisely in 1863 with the discovery of a quartzite hand axe from laterite bed near Madras in the peninsular part of India by Robert Bruce Foote, a British geologist. Although a Frenchman called Le Mesurier found a Neolithic Celt from Uttar Pradesh in India, the first prehistoric implement discovered, but it was Bruce Foote who made systematic study of prehistoric artifacts together with the geological context of the finds. Throughout his carrier as a geologist in India he carried out his work until his death in 1912. The foundation for prehistoric studies in India was laid down by Bruce Foote.

Farther work on prehistory started with the establishment of the department of anthropology in the University of Calcutta in 1920. Since then scholars like P. Mitra, H.C. Das Gupta, L. Cammiade, M.C. Burkitt, F.J. Richards, K.R. Todd and many others contributed to the prehistoric studies. The Yale-Cambridge expedition (1939) in the Indian subcontinent may be considered as a landmark in the field of Indian prehistory. The expedition was headed by H. de Terra, T.T. Paterson and T. de Chardin. They conducted intensive survey work on the Quaternary geology and associated cultural remains from undivided India. The expedition had inducted two young scholars from India, D. Sen and V.D. Krishnaswamy, who on their own right contributed to the advancement of prehistoric study. Universities like Calcutta, Baroda, Pune and others, as well as, Department of Archaeology, Government of India carried out research in prehistory. Outstanding work had been done by the Postgraduate institute of Archaeology, Deccan College, Pune, under the guidance of H.D. Sankalia. Scholars from different parts of India were trained at Deccan College, who has enriched the knowledge on prehistory of India. Throughout the twentieth century a large number of scholars in different parts of India worked relentlessly on prehistoric studies.

Twenty first century began with substantial accumulation of data on prehistory. Work which began with surface finds emerged as full-fledged research work on prehistoric culture and its makers. Researches brought to light proper Indian terminological concepts for Stone Age cultures in India. Sequential ordering of culture came into existence with the development of absolute and geo-chronological as well as palaeo-environmental framework. Understanding of specific problems in relation to human behaviour emerged. Indian prehistory suffers from the lack of fossil remains of the makers of the culture except for the lone calvarium of Narmada man. Methodology applied for such studies are multidisciplinary in nature. In spite of the large scale research there are still a good amount of lacunae in the knowledge of prehistory. Limitations are with availability of absolute dates, proper identification of stratigraphy and sediments, standardized classification of finished, unfinished, debitage and other related materials from either primary or secondary context in relation to geological and absolute time scale. With this background in mind the colloquium had been proposed. The International Union for Prehistoric and Protohistoric Sciences (UISPP) is an appropriate platform for assessing the status of prehistoric studies in the twenty first century in India and for formulating strategies for future research.

A total of twenty abstracts of papers for presentation in the colloquium were received, though ultimately nine persons could be present for oral presentation. However, those papers covered a cross section of relevant research areas. Vidula Jaiswal made an assessment of the prehistoric research done so far in India. She put forth recommendation for farther progress in diverse areas of research. Asok Datta gave a discourse about his work on the Acheulian culture of West Bengal, especially along Gandheswari river valley. His approach to the study is through settlement system of Acheulian people. Bishnupriya Basak focused on the Mesolithic culture of West Bengal. Her work involved the study of landscape in relation to land use and resource utilization on the basis of spread of microliths at a site. For this she has taken help of modern theory and methodology. Jagannath N. Pal has pointed out the importance of middle Ganga valley and surrounding foothills of Vindhayas for the development of food production. He gave an elaborate account of findings from recently excavated Neolithic sites in the area. The area appears to have yielded evidence of food production as early in date as 6th to 5th millennium B.C. Experimental Archaeology is taken up in India for prehistoric studies in a limited scale. Krishnendu Polley, jointly with the present author, presented a paper on experiments in manufacturing of Paleolithic type of tools from quartz nodules. This raw material is used extensively for manufacturing tools in eastern India. Metal craft emerged in India in due course. India being a land of diversified culture has got some of the early cultural traits continuing even through present time. Falguni Chakraborty has deliberated upon the ancient tradition of brass working by means of lost wax process, which is still practiced by some groups of people. The methodology is worth mentioning as it throws light on and helps reconstruction of ancient metal craft. Rajendran found skull of a human baby in a ferricrete deposit. This is first evidence of recovery of human remains from ferricrete. Modern techniques were used for the study of the skull, which is still within the ferricrete. The skull dates back to middle Pleistocene. Sankhyan has also dealt with humanoid and human types from India. His work involved skeletal as well as molecular analysis of both ancient fossils and modern human groups respectively. Both Rajendran's and Sankhyan's papers point out to the makers of prehistoric culture in India. Finally Manoj K. Singh has raised vital question regarding future of prehistoric study in India. He emphasized on training students and scholars in methods and techniques of prehistoric studies. He farther cautioned against over specialization in the field of prehistoric studies.

Prehistoric study which started with much vigor in the twentieth century has lost some of its strength in recent years. India's cultural heritage is deep, indigenous and diversified. For proper understanding of the prehistoric background of India much more intensive research is needed with trained personnel, modern equipments, techniques and methods.

The authors, co-coordinators of the colloquium C01 are grateful to UISPP for the support provided for attending the conference and for bringing out the publication. Special gratitude is expressed for Professor Luiz Oosterbeek and his team of helpers for bringing a great success to the conference and making this publication a reality.

PREHISTORIC INDIA: ASSESSMENT & PROSPECTS IN THE TWENTY-FIRST CENTURY

Vidula JAYASWAL

Professor, Department of Ancient Indian History, Culture & Archaeology, BANARAS HINDU UNIVERSITY, *Varanasi-221005*, India. P 6 New Medical Enclave, Banaras Hindu University. Varanasi-221 005. Vidula.bhu@gmail.com, # (91)(0542)-369370

Abstract: *Similar to the history and growth of archaeology, the discipline of Stone Age studies in India is also governed primarily by the changing aims of investigations. This is well demonstrated in the historical stages through which this discipline has progressed. For example, the main stages in chronological sequence at the beginning was, - to locate sites and discover tools was to fulfill the aim to prepare the prehistoric map of the subcontinent, while, - extensive investigation at primary context and habitation locales, of the twenty[th] century revolves around reconstructing the behaviour in totality of the prehistoric man. Similarly, - recording the details of palaeo-climatic conditions, - the growing tendency to use scientific methods for the interpretation of the Stone Age data etc., are the efforts to achieve the aim to understand the ecological adaptation tendencies, technological attainments of the earliest human groups of India.*

An attempt is made in this paper to demonstrate the stage where Indian Prehistory has reached today. It is imperative to review the important researches carried out so far, and particularly in the twenty[th] century. Since the canvass of the proposed theme of this paper is very vast, only important examples have been selected for the purpose. Besides, due to the fact that, all the three stages of Stone Age - the Palaeolithic, Mesolithic and Neolithic, vary from one and other considerably in view of the content and nature of evidence, it is proposed to discuss all these stages individually. The prospective problems and inquiries which need attention of the Indian prehistorians in the twenty-first century, also forms an integral part of the proposed paper, and has been incorporated in the section following the brief historical right up.

Keywords: *Prehistoric-Archaeology, history, growth, review, stone ages, stages*

Résumé: *Tel que l'histoire et croissance de l'archéologie, la discipline des études sur l'Âge de la Pierre en Inde est aussi gouvernée par le changement des buts des recherches. Ceci est bien démontré par les étapes historiques a travers lesquelles la discipline a progressée. Par exemple, les stades principaux de sa séquence chronologique étaient, au début, de localiser des sites et découvrir des outils, pour accomplir le but de préparer la carte préhistorique du sous-continent, alors que des recherches extensives sur des contextes primaires et des habitats, au XXème siècle, portent sur la reconstruction du comportement de l'homme préhistorique. De même façon, les registres en détail des conditions paléo-climatiques, la tendance croissante a utiliser des méthodes scientifiques d'interprétation des données sur l'Âge de la Pierre, etc., sont des efforts pour atteindre une connaissance des tendances d'adaptation écologique et des acquis technologiques des premiers groupes humains en Inde.*

Un essai est fait dans cet article pour démontrer le stade auquel la Préhistoire Indienne est arrivée. C'est impératif de réviser les importantes recherches qui ont été entreprises, en particulier au XXème siècle. Vu que la portée de ce thème est très vaste, seul des exemples importants furent sélectionnés a ce propos. Aussi, vu que tous les trois stades de l'Âge de la Pierre – Paléolithique, Mésolithique, Néolithique – varient beaucoup sur le contenu et la nature des évidences, on se propose de les discuter individuellement. Les problèmes prospectifs et les enquêtes qui requièrent l'attention des préhistoriens Indiens dans le XXIème siècle forment aussi une partie intégrale de l'article et sont incorporés dans la section qui se suit à un bref historique.

Mots clés: *Archéologie Préhistorique, histoire, développement, âge de la pierre*

Similar to the history and growth of archaeology, the discipline of Stone Age studies in India is governed primarily with the changing aims of investigations. To mention some of the main stages in chronological sequence are – attempt to finding the tools and discovering Stone Age sites, – to locating primary contexts of habitations, – recording the details of palaeo-climatic conditions, – the growing tendency to use scientific methods for the interpretation of the Stone Age data etc. Since the canvass of the proposed theme of this paper is very vast, it may not be possible to provide a full narrative account of all the researches, which have been carried out so far, in this continent. Thus, an attempt is first made to demonstrate the stage where Indian Prehistory has reached today, through important selective examples. And, the prospective problems to be taken into account for the prehistoric researches for the twenty-first century, thereafter. Since all the three stages of Stone Age – the Palaeolithic, Mesolithic and Neolithic, vary from one and other considerably, it is imperative to discuss all these stages individually for a meaningful assessment.

THE PALAEOLITHIC PERIOD

The Palaeolithic studies in India has a history which is only a little more than thirty years younger than that of Europe, where the stone tools of the Palaeolithic period were assigned for the first time as workmanship of the early man. Since 1986 the time assigned for the beginning of the early Stone Age studies in India, there has been continuous growth in this discipline. The entire period of the Palaeolithic researches in India, on account of the aim and emphasis on the investigation tendency may broadly be divided into the four following stages.

STAGE I: In the first stage, – from 1863 when B. Foote discovered the cleaver at Pallavaram (Foote, B. 1914), – to about the first quarter of the twentieth century – the aim of prehistory was to bring to light as many sites on the map of India as possible. As a result of this, prehistoric potentiality of a number of regions of India such as Uttar Pradesh, Rajasthan, Andhra and Tamilnadu etc., could be identified. This stage provided foundation to the study of Stone Age archaeology in India.

STAGE II: While the discoveries of Palaeoliths continued in some other areas as in Bombay presidency and in the north western, central and southern parts of the subcontinent, the emphasis was lain also on the palaeo-climatic reconstructions in this stage. This period can be identified as the era of systematic studies. The attempt was to study the artifacts within the geo-chronological frame of the sedimentary sequence. Along with these field studies there were attempts to correlate the Pleistocene sediments of various regions, – the Potwar sequence was place at par with that of the Narmada valley (De Terra & Paterson. 1935) on one hand, – and on the other, on account of the techno-typological considerations various cultural traditions of the Palaeolithic epoch, – "Madrasian" and "Soanian" cultures of the north-west and the south regions, were identified (Krishnaswamy. 1938). These attempts initiated a strong tradition of techno-typological studies and palaeo-climatic reconstructions, in the Palaeolithic studies.

STAGE III: This stage of Palaeolithic researches in India witnessed extensive search for both, – the human activities and the evidence for palaeo-cliamate. This was the era of river valley survey, which was initiated by the discoveries in Gujarat (Zeuner.F.1950), and was followed by Sankalia and his team of students, and Sen and his students during fifties and sixties of the twentieth century. The main contribution of this stage was to identify individual techno-cultural stages of the Palaeolithic period. For instance, "Nevasian Culture", the Middle Palaeolithic tool tradition was recognized at Nevasa in a separate horizon than the Lower Palaeolithic (Sankalia. 1954). Besides, the Pleistocene sequence of particularly peninsula seem to form a definite pattern in terms of tool bearing horizons of Gravels I & II, and the intermediary silts which were devoid of implements. These deposits were believed to represent wet and dry cycles of the Pleistocene epoch prevalent in the tropical region of this sub-continent. Needless to mention that the investigations carried in this phase were important for locating all the main areas which retained remains of one Palaeolithic period. However, in course of interpretation of sedimentary sequence of tool bearing horizons there was a tendency to over simplify the complex sediment-sequences. Also the practice to use a number of sets of terminologies for the prehistoric stages, such as – Early, Middle and Late Stone Ages, – Series I, II and III, – "Core cultures", "Flake cultures" and "Blade cultures", became prevalent, which till late created confusion particularly in the minds of young researchers.

STAGE IV: Period from seventies to the end of twentieth century, was significant for the Indian Palaeolithic studies in more than one ways. For, not only scientific methods were adopted at large scale for the study of Early Man in view to the palaeo-climatic reconstructions, but also attention of the investigators was diverted to a number of cultural aspects, – such as technological skills, dwelling tendencies, adaptive capacities to an environmental zone etc. Since this is the stage, which is directly responsible for the formation of the current status, it may be worthy while to enumerate briefly, the important researches of this period.

Recognition of Upper Palaeolithic in proper geo-chronological context in Belan Valley in Uttar Pradesh, was one of the most important discoveries of the seventies (Sharma, G.R. 1973). Since, as a result of this it was possible to demarcate and identify all the three techno-cultural stages of the Palaeoloithic period in India. With the recognition of the Upper Palaeolithic, there were other confident identification of remains of this period from other parts, such as Andhra (Murty, M.L.K. 1969) and Maharashtra (Sali, S.A. 1970), but it was also possible to finally put a full top to the long debate on terminologies. The justification for the adoption of the Palaeolithic-Mesolithic set was accepted. Needless to mention that this shift has certainly given firmer grounds for the identification and interpretation of the Stone Age cultures and evaluate the Indian evidence at par with the global scenario of the Early Man.

The field studies of seventies and eighties of the last century proved particularly rewarding for the reconstruction of the behaviour of the Acheulian Man in India. This is well demonstrated by the discoveries of primary context sites like Hunsgi (Paddayya, K. 1982) and Paisra (Pant, P.C. & Jayaswal, V. 1991). The field records at these sites are not only very meticulous, but, the evidence has been extensively interpreted through application of various ethnographic models. At Hunsgi valley in Andhrra Pradesh, for instance, the investigator could reconstruct Acheulian settlement system, through the reconstruction of the interrelationship between the Food resources, and the Adaptive role of the lithic industry, and in turn working out such possibilities as dry and wet season strategies on one hand, and home range, social organization and demographic considerations of the Acheulian dweller, on the other (Paddyya, K. 1982: 61-95).

The evidence unearthed at Paisra in Bihar, is unique in more than one ways. Since it is the first site of the Indo-Pak subcontinent which has revealed clear indications for the construction of shelters by the Acheulian inhabitants of the Kharagpur valley. Besides, it is also marked by a large series and different kinds of shelters, remains of which are found from a number of localities in the form of post-holes and the stone alignments. Besides, choice of the dwelling places and the camp-base and resource base strategies could also be determined at this site. It was clear from the archaeological remains of Paisra valley that this region was a favourite resort of late/advanced Acheulian times. This is because the valley had sufficient food, particularly during rainy season and post rains. For which the areas around the present tribal village was inhabited time and again by small groups of nomadic food collectors. Not only the dwelling locales were selected carefully, – the flat and higher places of the valley, – but protective devices were also being constructed to facilitate living. Construction of temporary shelters with the help of floral components plenty in the area, also were supported by stone alignments or erecting post/posts. These shelters could be reconstructed through ethnological models of the hunter-gatherers. A complete format of the day to day activities of the early dwellers could further be reconstructed by determining various activity spots, which are grouped under – camp-base and resource-base activities. The refuge resulting from both of these categories are distinct and form varying archaeological patterns. For example, sporadic scatter of artifacts, which are found almost in the entire Paisra valley in about a radius of 10 sq km, could be determined as food and raw material collecting zone. While the dense concentration of artefact-scatters along with the remains of shelters clustering around the village of Paisra, could be recognize as camp-base zone. The camp-base zone besides retaining evidence for shelters or the resting areas, also had such spots where tools were fabricated and food processed.

Archaeological records human behavior though have come to light for Acheulian stage, the same could not be retrieved for the successive stages of the Palaeolithic epoch.

For example, though many sites have been discovered and some of these were also excavated, the picture of the Middle Palaeolithic India remains more or less vague. This is because most of the sites are either surface finds or river valley sites. In case of such sites which may be identified as dwelling locales, – like the rock-shelter site of Bhimbetka,– the nature of collection is such that a clear-cut distinction between the Acheulian and the Middle Palaeolithic is difficult to make. Search for primary context sites of Middle Palaeolithic phase, thus is necessary. A similar situation is also viewed in case of the Upper Palaeolithic remains.

Techno-typological studies for palaeolithic collections, which are often not spoken highly by some of the archaeologists, need to be discussed in this forum. For, as a method of scientific study it's utility is advantageous, in many ways, – classification of collections into technological groups and cultures, placing tool-kits into chronological sequence, resulting into relative dating etc. Besides, for determining the subsistence activities of the Stone Age man, – working capacity or utility of the tools, –and even physical capacity of the maker could also be assessed by this methodology. This method after initial scrutiny of the data, opens up, many enquiries which are related to the subsistence, dwelling tendencies and a

complete understanding of the life of the Pleistocene man. For instance, it could be noticed that the Middle Palaeolithic tool-kits in India, in general, are devoid of very finely made tools of Mousterian tradition (Jayaswal, V. 1978). Developed technologies and effective tools made on flakes detached in various forms after preparation of cores, has been identified as the technological attainment of the *Homo-Neanderthelensis,* the species of Early Man, who is known to have almost equal cranial capacity to the modern man. Instead the Indian Middle Palaeolithic appears to be a tradition in which the tendency to make serrated edges and notches on the working edge was dominant. A case study of techno-typological features of Indian collections indicates that Middle Palaeolithic collections have very dominant proportion of denticulated and notched flakes and scrapers, which is comparable to the Mousterian of Denticulate tradition of Western Europe (Pant, P.C. & V. Jayawal.1978). Similarly, there is strikingly low proportion or absence of pointed tools, –good points made on triangular flakes or Levallois and Mousterian points, in the Indian collections (Jayaswal, V. 197). However, one does find some borers in the collection with short working edges prepared by alternate retouch. The questions, which need to be attended to, at priority basis, therefore, are two fold. One, – finding and identifying the author/authors of the Middle Palaeolithic culture/cultures of India, and the other, – the possible mode of subsistence and day to day activity of the Middle Palaeolithic man in India.

Likewise, the Upper Palaeolithic phase, though could be recognized with certainty, the collections brought to light are limited and mostly characterized by nonspecific tools. A poor technological attainment during this period is also reflected by the collections, specially when compared with those of the findings in Europe. It is also required that an explanation is sought for the conspicuous absence for the prevalence of developed blade technology and the tools made on blades. It may be held that the studies of the Upper Palaeolithic phase in India is still far from satisfactory. For, not only the findings are very limited, but also the nature of the collections and the contexts of the habitation deposits are poorly represented. The non-specific nature and tendency for notching and denticulation of edges of tools, continue from the earlier phase to this stage also, which instead of flakes now are made on blades and bladelets. As a result, the conspicuous absence of well made blade tools, like knives, pointed tools, burins etc., is glaring in the tool-kits of this sub-continent. In stead occurrence of bladelets and microliths form integral part of most of the Upper Palaeolithic collection of India which have come to light recently from proper geo-chronological contexts (Sharma, G.R. & Clark, J.D. 1983 and Pant, P.C. 1982). The question one faces in this case also revolves around the physical capacity of the man of the end of the Pleistocene, and also the possible relationship of adaptation of ecology, vis-à-vis technological skills. It may be recalled that it has been shown through the scrutiny of the global data that around 18.000 BP, "in the southern hemisphere, environmental selection on behaviour is regarded as a powerful and dynamic explanation for changes in the archaeological records" (Gamble, C. & O. Soffer. 1990). If Microliths are accepted as an effort to the adaptation of the arid conditions, which they appear to be, is it not possible that their occurrence in the Upper Palaeolithic tool-bearing deposits evidence the tendency to adapt the new changes in the environmental conditions during terminal Pleistocene? Utility of microlithic technology to arid condition's subsistence is amply demonstrated in the archaeological records, which has been discussed below.

THE MESOLITHIC PERIOD

The early discoveries of Microliths or the "Pigmy tools", which have been identified as the diagnostic techno-typological trait of the Mesolithic, also go back to as early as the middle of the nineteenth century, as the finding was made by A.C. Carlleyle (Smith, V.A. 1906). Since then due to continuous discoveries of microlithic sites not only the collections have grown richer by day, but, it is also clear that except for colder zones, like the Kashmir valley and the very humid area of the northeastern India, almost all the ecological zones were under occupation by the users of pigmy tools in India. Quite a good number of habitation sites in various contexts, – rock-shelter, sand-dune, river valley, open area plateau, horse-shoe-lake side, etc., have also been excavated. As a result of which it is possible to reconstruct the Mesolithic life in comparatively better way than the earlier phase. In spite of this the traits of Mesolithic becomes often not very distinct, due to long continuation of microliths.

Though microliths may be identified as the diagnostic trait of the Mesolithic stage, their occurrence is not restricted to the Mesolithic period only. It has long history, in which Mesolithic is one, but a significant section. I have identified eight different culture contexts in which these pigmy tools occur. These are – The Upper Palaeolithic, the 'Epi-Palaeolithic', the Early Mesolithic, the Late Mesolithic, the Neolithic, the Chalcolithic, the early Iron Age, and the isolated post-Mesolithic Microlithic Cultures (Jayaswal, V. 1997: 37). These stages for general discussions may be divided into four major techno-culture stages, – the pre-Mesolithic, the Mesolithic, the post-Mesolithic: stages of technological developments, and, the post-Mesolithic: Microlithic Culture. Needless to mention that contribution of each of the stage is significant in the history of microlithic technology. In view of formulation, prevalence and technological status, these stages could be identified as, – Stage of Innovation, Stage of Formative theme, Stage of Survival and Stage of Conservatism, and follow the successive order of the geo-chronology (Jayaswal, V. 1997: 35-49).

STAGE I: Innovation – The appearance and earliest existence of microliths in Uttar Pradesh is in association with the full-fledged blade industries of the Upper Palaeolithic period (Pant, P.C. 1982: 101-102). The techno-typological attributes borne by microliths, as was discussed earlier, indicate that this technocratic group was modification and development over the blade technology. The beginnings of microlith-making in Belan and Son valleys are dateable to *circa* twenty-fourth millennium BC. The archaeological remains from Gravel III of the Belan-Seoti valley and the later Pleistocene deposits of the Son valley (Sharma G.R. & J.D. Clark. 1983), indicate that the Upper Palaeolithic industries which are datable by the Radiocarbon method between 24, 000 and 18,000 BC, are associated with microliths. It is interesting to note that right from the beginning when pigmy tools formed only 10 % of the total implement collection, the microlithic technology appears in developed form, – the specimens are made on well made bladelets (micro-blade having less than 12 mm width), and characterized by abruptly retouched side/sides,– two morphological distinctions for identifications of a typical microlith. But the forms of implements are mostly non-specific. For, the tool-kit is dominated by backed bladelets and presence of a few lunates. Such perfect geometric forms as triangle and trapeze are either absent or when present, as is the case with triangles, these are in negligible proportion and mostly of atypical form. It therefore, is possible to summarize that making of microliths emerged as a subordinate trait to the full-fledged blade based industries, during the terminal Pleistocene. It may further be held that, the *origin of this techno-culture trait, was an innovation and not an invention or diffusion*, in Uttar Pradesh, where it's earliest context is well documented (Jayaswal,V.1997: 38).

STAGE II: Formative theme – The archaeological remains of the post-Pleistocene and the earlier part of the Holocene are dominated by microliths. This technocratic group not only appears to have formed diagnostic culture trait, but also seems to have multiple growth in the form of variety of non-specific and specific implement types. The blade element and blade-based tools gave way to microliths and recessed to the subordinate position. In archaeological reports the reminiscents of this stage are recorded as 'Epi-Palaeolithic', 'Early Mesolithic'and 'Advanced Mesolithic/Proto-Neolithic' (Sharma, G.R. *et.al.*1980: 33-76).

The stone tool collection which, succeeds the Upper Palaeolithic industries in Belan valley has been identified by the investigators as that of the 'Epi-Palaeolithic' stage (Sharma, G.R. *et.al.*1980: 37). The 'Epi-Palaeolithic, Chopani-mando Phase I, appears to have Early Mesolithic characteristics. For, not only microliths became very pronounced (up to 80 % of the finished tools in collections), but, germs of semi-sedentism, in the form of post-holes and the floors have been noted in the associated deposits.

It may be put to record that such alluvial plains were suitable region for the formulation of the Mesolithism, which were situated in the vicinity of the hills. Evidence from Belan is a demonstrative example of this. But, gradually the alluvial eco-zones lying at a distance from the hills were also fully exploited. This hypothesis is based on the wide distribution of Mesolithic sites in the middle Ganga plains. About two hundred sites have been located in the Sultanpur, Pratapgarh and Varanasi districts of Uttar Pradesh (Sharma, G.R. *et.al.*1980: 123-131). This group of sites suggests short duration occupation of the plains, rich in food resources. The evidence unearthed at Sarai-nahar-rai, Damdama and Mahadaha, clearly demonstrates that the sides of horseshoe-lakes were the preferred habitats of these hunter-gatherers, who appear to have been attracted to the alluvial eco-system. Savanah-type of grass cover with patches of deciduous forests and small pools of water in the form of horse-shoe-lakes and small rivers were the geographical features, which appear to be attracting Mesolithic population in this region. The attraction of alluvial ecology was so strong that, even the scarcity of raw material in this region was not felt as a serious drawback. It was overcome by a long distance transportation of raw material, – from the Vindhyan hills. Besides, bone and antler were also used as substitute media for tools, to overcome this draw back. Use of bone and antler tools at Sarai-nahar-rai is significant. Though middle Ganga plain was the most suitable habitat of this time, some other alluvial patches which formed parts of the Son and the Damodar valleys were also under occupation (Sharma, G.R. & J. D. Clark. 1983; Lal, B.B. 1958).

The subsistence of this time appears to have strong tendency for hunting, which is evident from the faunal remains of the excavated sites. The wild species of animals identified at the horse-shoe-lake sites include big and small animals and good amount of aquatic creatures. It is also significant to note that use of pots and heavy-duty tools, large amount of cereal consumption was perhaps still not under practice. But elements of semi-sedentism are evident in the remains of shelters. At Chopani-mando, seven huts were unearthed in Phase II. While at Sarai-nahar-rai post-holes and remains of floors indicate construction of shelters of more temporary nature (Sharma, G.R. *et al.* 1980: 33-37& 140). The size and location of hearths, at Sarai-nahar-rai, suggest community living and somewhat organized behaviour. The evidence for burying the dead in and around the settlement area was perhaps indication of patterned social behaviour.

On account of the Radiocarbon dates from Sarai-nahar-rai (8395 ± 110 BC) and Bagor II (6380 ± 220 BC), it may be held that between ninth and seventh millennium BC (Sharma, G.R. *et al.* 1980; Sharma, G.R. & J.D. Clark. 1983), not only did the microliths acquired status of formative theme, but this techno-cultural trait may be accepted as identification of the Mesolithism in archaeological records (Jayaswal, V. 1997: 40). It may be emphasized that parallel to microliths, there is no other culture trait such as pottery or significant heavy-duty tool, which can be ascertained as yardstick for recognizing this techno-economic stage. Soon after the microlith-dominated subsistence was well adapted in the alluvial

eco-system of the middle Ganga plain, it appears to undergo change. This change was in terms of a major shift from hunting-gathering strategies to incipient food producing economy. A few new technologies such as potting and ground stone tool making were also initiated, which along with the new mode of subsistence was a major breakthrough in the history of this region. This process of transformation shall be discussed a little later with Neolithic stage.

It needs to be mentioned that the post-Mesolithic occurrence of microliths falls within two categories,– one which continued with the main line of techno-cultural progress, the other, which survived in isolation as the dominant culture trait. The earlier catergory has been identified by this author, – 'Stage of Survival', while the latter as, – 'Stage of Conservatism'. Scrutiny of Radiocarbon dates and the contemporary archaeological findings from various Microlithic, Neolithic and Chalcolithic sites of southern Uttar Pradesh and Madhya Pradesh indicates that it was around six millennium BC, these two culture-setups drifted from one and the other.

STAGE III: Survivalt – The archaeological remains dating between sixth millennium BC, and the early Christian era belongs to three technological stages, the Neolithic, the Chalcolithic and the early Iron Age. In this category, microlithic technology seems to exist parallel, but subordinate to the advanced technologies, which formed the basis for the Neolithic, Chalcolithic and Iron Age cultures.

STAGE IV: Conservatism – This category survived as a parallel branch to the main stream of culture growth discussed earlier. Since microliths are the most prominent culture trait of this group of cultures, it has been named by me – the 'Microlithic Culture'. The attitude to cling to the microlithic technology and the resistance towards change is so strong in this case, that, it reflects conservative attitude of the culture makeup. This cultural conservatism is further marked by the tendency to confine to the geographically isolated areas, – like the periphery of western deserts lying in Gujarat and Rajasthan, and hills of Vindhya-Kaimur systems (Jayaswal, V. 1997: 43-45).

Scrutiny of Radiocarbon dates from the microlithic deposits of various rock-shelters of the region indicates that Microlithic Culture of the Vindhyan-Kaimur region had survived for about five to six thousand years. The date from Adamgarh (5500 ± 130 BC) is noteworthy, as it is so far the earliest date for the Microlithic Culture. On account of which sixth/fifth millennium BC, may be ascertained as the beginning for the Microlithic Culture. Similarly, the dates obtained from Bhimbetka, help fixing the end of this date – bracket to around 1500 BC (Jayaswal, V. 1997: 45). It's late survival in restricted parts might even have continued up to the historical period, *circa* A.D. 1000 (date from Bhimbetka of (950 ±110 Bp).

The Vindhyan Microlithic Cultures may be divided within two chrono-cultural stages. It's earlier stage, appears to date between sixth and third millennium BC. Marked by pastoralism, – one of the Neolithic subsistence, this culture stream appears an intrusion from the neighbour-hood, – alluvial plains. The later stage which post-dates 2500 BC, is marked by borrowed elements of Chalcolithic and Iron Age cultures of the plains. In the early phase of Microlithic Culture, though hunting was practiced, evidence for animal husbandry is also pronounced. The faunal remains from Bagor and Adamgarh sites suggest that both, – hunting and domestication of animals formed the basis for the subsistence of this culture. Besides, the rock paintings depict a number of hunting scenes. Nomadic tendency in which large rock-shelters were occupied as the epi-centres of dwelling activities, was perhaps another noteworthy culture trait of the Vindhya-Kaimur Microlithic Culture. The thick habitation *debris* unearthed from the rock-shelters at Adamgarh (Joshi, R.V. 1978) and Laharia-dih (Pant, P.C. 1982), support this presumption. As undisrupted microlithic habitation deposits have been exposed at these sites. The tendency to occupy natural shelters and not to built huts for habitation was the dwelling tendency of the Microlith using communities occupying the hilly terrain.

In the early phase of Microlithic Culture, though hunting was practiced, evidence for animal husbandry is also pronounced. The faunal remains from Bagor and Adamgarh sites suggest that both the hunting and domestication of animals formed the basis for subsistence of cultural tradition. The ratio between the wild and domesticated animals from living refuge noted at Adamgarh is 1:1 (Joshi, R.V. 1978:38). The identified species, the one humped cattle, buffalo, goat/sheep *etc.*, indicate herding for food resources.

The hunting gathering way of life aided with pastoralism persisted during the later phase of the Microlithic Culture also. Besides nomadism, which was essential for hunting-gathering, as well as the pastoral economy in the hills, short duration occupation of large rock-shelters also continued in the later phase. Microliths also remained the basic technological trait till the end. During the entire time-span geometric microliths along with the other unspecified forms survived as the main techno-cultural trait, which except for some frequency fluctuations remained more or less unaltered. Other culture traits such as heavy-duty tools may or may not be found. But, a limited number of pots are invariably associated with these finds. It may be mentioned that both hand-made and wheel-made pots have been retrieved from the habitations. The former appears to be the local production, while the later was imported articles. The well fired and wheel turned pottery mirrors the techno-cultural levels identified as the Neolithic, Chalcolithic and Iron Ages of the neighbourhood. In the process of borrowing of pots such articles as copper and iron implements, glass bangles and beads *etc.*, were also obtained by the rock-shelter dwellers of the Vindhya-Kaimur region. It may,

therefore, be held that there was a close interaction in terms of exchange of goods between the authors of the Microlithic culture and the other contemporary communities of the Ganga plains. It is important to note, that in spite of the awareness of technological progress of the neighbourhood the Microlith-using communities of the hills preferred to cling to the old ways of living. I have identified this situation as a tribal character (Jayaswal, V. 1997).

THE NEOLITHIC PERIOD

The initial discovery of a ground stone axe in the year 1842 (Sankalia, H.D. 1962:152) was followed by a number of surface findings of stone celts in Chhotanagpur plateau east India and Deccan. The excavations of Neolithic sites of sixties to eighties of the twentieth century revealed proper habitation deposits of the early pastoral and agricultural communities in various parts of the country. In this venture specific regions could be demarcated for Neolithic remains. As the evidence stands today, findings under the category of Neolithic remains appear to confine to small regional pockets. In the light of the findings these regions were identified from four (Thapar, B.K. 1965) to six (Thapar, B.K. 1985: 25). The north and north-western part of the Indian sub-continent falling now out side the boundaries of modern India, is, however, excluded from the present theme. The Neolithic remains of which are very different from the rest of the regions, and appears to form extension of the west Asian complex, both with regard to the time frame and the settlement tendency. The remaining six nucleus regions of India are marked by cultural diversities. As each region has different story to tell both with regard to the culture contents and chronology. But, the evidence for the origins of Neolithic way of life and subsistence has been brought to light from the middle Gang plain which is adjacent to the Vindhyan foot hills (Sharma, G.R. *et al.* 1980).

The foot hills of Vindhyas which is drained by Belan river system was the area where Neolithic subsistence originated. The twin geological compositions – the hills and the fertile alluvial plains, were the most apt ecological conditions for this instance. Besides suitable eco-system this region also had an advantage of having successive stages of Stone Age cultures, which provided desired culture background. The culmination of hunting-gathering subsistence, for instance, was reached in the form of Mesolithic by six millennium B.C. in this region. Late Mesolithic phase, which is also referred to as 'Proto-Neolithic', of this region, suggests transition between the hunting-gathering and the food producing economies. For example, some of the food processing equipments and the tendency of semi-sedentism, which were acquired during the Late Mesolithic phase marked the beginning of Neolithic traits. This evidence has been brought to light from Chopani-mando. Archaeological remains of Koldihwa and Mahgarha mark the later stage, when food producing subsistence had taken deep roots. Not only the lithic requirements for the tools could be fulfilled locally but, the alluvial plains and the forests provided domesticated varieties of plants and animal species. It may be noted that the knowledge about the domesticated varieties of flora and fauna was already acquired by the end of the mature phase of Mesolithic. It is therefore, logical to assume that the initiation and formulation of food producing stage in Belan valley was completely in accordance with the ecological factors and also adaptive qualities and technological skills acquired by the indigenous habitants of the Vindhya-Belan region.

The shift in the subsistence was aided by new technological inventions. For instance heavy-duty tools were needed for agriculture, construction of protective devices and processing of cereals. The semi-sedentary occupational tendency was progressing towards sedentary way of life. The settlements needed good amount of carpenter's tools. Microliths could not meet all these requirements satisfactorily. The new technology which emerged from these necessities was 'ground/polished tool' making. Axes dominate the tool-kit, while the other carpenter's tools such as adze, chisel etc., also farewell. Large blocks of hard stones were selected for these implements. After achieving main shape, the surfaces were grounded for the purpose of acquiring hardness and durability. Small tools were made on bone and antlers also. The other main requirement of the food production stage was the storing of access edibles. This perhaps gave rise to potting technology. Hand-made ill-fired pots of Khakhi and grey colours of the period were though crude and preliminary as far as the potting technology is concerned, these were decorated with cord impression and also at times painted with ochre colour. Making of earthen pots appears to be an inventive trait. But, the utility of earlier tools like microliths also continued side by side.

The archaeological remains unearthed at Koldihwa and Mahagarha indicate village like settlement. The hut dwellings were associated with pens of domesticated animals (Sharma, G.R. et al. 1980). The hoof-marks of cattle and goats exposed at Koldihwa confirms that pastoralism was one of the main subsistence. Incipient farming is represented by single crop rice cultivation. The archaeological context and the Radiocarbon dates obtained from the Belan valley indicates that Neolithic stage prevailed in this region between circa sixth and third millennium B.C.

The subsistence based on domestication of plants and animals would logically have resulted in sufficient food for the early communities of Belan region. Such a situation gives impetus to the growth of population. With incipient farming and less perfect pastoralism there always is stress on natural resources. It may be argued therefore, that the growth of Neolithic population in the Belan valley had lessened the natural resources over a span of time. Thus, some of the indigenous inhabitants were compelled to migrate to other regions. Foot hills of Kaimur ranges in south Bihar appears to be one zone

which had somewhat similar ecological conditions with which Koldihwians were familiar. Chain of settlements discovered by Birendra Pratap Singh of our Department, in Kaimur and Rohtas districts, in Bihar, indicates that a good section of Belan valley population moved towards east, and found ecology of the new region akin to the one they were used to. The knowledge of food production, both, the plant and animal species for the domestication were brought to this region from their home-land. For, some time these pastoral and farming groups continued to retain the original traits and subsistence of Koldihwan culture. As, farming of only one variety of rice was still in incipient stage. And, so were the under developed crafts. This was the stage of settling down in this new region. Evidence obtained by the excavations at Senuwar provides grounds for such a reconstruction (Singh, B.P. 2004). The Radiocarbon date (2200 BC) obtained from Period IA, at this site indicates that this wave of migration in the Kaimur region took place around the first half of the third millennium BC. On stratigraphic considerations the stage of settling in this region appears to persist for about a couple of centuries.

It is significant to note that, in the late Neolithic period, Senuwarians developed cultural contacts with communities of far distance places. Noteworthy communities were the civilized Harappans of the north-west and the cattle breeders of the Deccan. Though the cultural impact of the south Indian Neolithic groups is partly reflected in pots and pans, contribution of the Harappans is glaring. This is evident in the form of sudden shift from the cultivation of one variety of rice to multiple crop farming. As was discussed above, all the new farmed species of the later half of the Period IA, at Senuwar, have been identified as Harappan cultivated varieties by Saraswat. Harappan cultural affinities are also demonstrated from typology of some of the pots. Whether the advanced agricultural practices traveled to the region understudy as technological knowledge or migration of people is difficult to ascertain at present. Nevertheless, it may be postulated that, since the alluvial ecology was a strong supporting factor in Rohtas region, it was possible to adopt the new agricultural system.

It was an imperative to have stretches of fertile land for the new agricultural practices. This requirement appears to have prompted Neolithic inhabitants to move towards inland of alluvial plains in south Bihar. It may not be a mere co-incidence that, the thick alluvial plain of Bihar is dotted with many early historical sites, most of which have late Neolithic horizons at the base. Double cropping cultivation, pastoralism and some hunting-gathering were the modes of subsistence which spread with these migratory groups. Along with the typical Neolithic traits, Harappan impact on particularly pots was part of this culture-package. Needless to mention that, ecology of middle Ganga plain was very suitable for the sustenance of the late Neolithic stage, which as a natural growth of cultures, subsequently developed into cultures of the Chalcolithic and early Iron ages.

The picture of cattle breeders of the Kashmir valley has a different pattern. The Neolithic remains unearthed in this region reveal two types of settlements. One, which is represented by Gufkral, Burzoham and Kanispur, appear to be camp-base settlements with long duration occupation *debris*. The high altitude location (between 1800 and 1600 m) of these sites would indicate that these were experiencing cold climatic conditions during the winters. While the other sites such as, – Ror, Dera-Gopipur and Baroli in Kngra Valley, not only were of low altitude locales (400 to 460 m), but are also of short duration occupation of the ancient pastorals (Manorj Kumar. 2004: 223). Also it could be interpreted from the sites of high altitudes, such as Kiari, that the sites of Ladakh were summer encampments of Neolithic groups. These sites appear to reveal trans human seasonal migrations in search of pastures for their animals. Detailed study of the archaeological remains and its comparison with tribal model, further suggested that though main subsistence of the pastoral communities of Kashmir, both the ancient and the present, is animal stocking, yet, incipient agriculture is also in practice. The cereals cropped were wheat, barley, pea and *masur* in the early stage and paddy in the later stage. But, the mode of agriculture was not advanced (Sharma, A.K. 1991). As cultivation in this case appears to be sowing a number of seeds in one patch of land en route seasonal migrations. This is done in the process of trans human movements from base camps to the pastures. The crops grow in accordance with their required time of maturity, which accordingly are reaped by the cultivator in stages. Thus, cultivation of a number of cereals during third millennium B.C. in Kashmir valley perhaps was the rudimentary way of incipient farming and not the developed form of multi crop cultivation (Manoj K. 2004: 229). Both the time-span and archaeological findings of Kashmir Neolithic further suggest that perhaps there were pastoral communities in the Sindh and Baluchistan regions which were contemporary to the city dwellers of Harappan times. And due to population pressure and/or scarcity of pastures, these communities were forced to move towards other regions. Kashmir valley was one, which had almost similar ecology with which these animal breeders were familiar. This hypothesis, gets further support from the fact that Mesolithic phase is completely absent in Kashmir.

Similarly, the Eastern Indian sites lack good archaeological deposits and make study vague. The nature of the sites like Sarutaru, Deojalihandi etc., could reveal small duration settlement which in tribal practice is related to the *jhum* cultivation. And very restricted amount of daily utility items found in the archaeological investigations, similarly could be indication that articles made of bamboo and wood were mostly in used (Manoj K. 2004: 239-40). In the absence of Mesolithic phase in eastern region, migration of Neolithic groups in the region could be another logical conjecture. The dates of these migrations needs to be ascertained.

The cattle breeding communities of Deccan have attracted attention of archaeologists since sixties of the last century (Allchin, B. & R. Allchin. 1982). In view of the dates though this group fall apart from being true Neolithic, the culture make up corresponds more or less with the pastoral subsistence aided by agriculture. Agriculture produce, in this region also includes a number of serials. The history of these communities is yet to be ascertained. For, the question of local origin or migration of food producing economy in Deccan is important to attend.

The above examples suggest that attempts have been made to reconstruct the life of the early farming and pastoral communities in general terms. It is unfortunate that detailed reports of some of the important excavated sites are not available, which obviously hampers the proper scrutiny of archaeological findings, and in turn restrict explanatory processes. The most important issue, which is open for debate, is the late to very late dates for the Neolithic remains in India. The initial inquiry one faces with regard to this is that, when the dates for particular techno-subsistent stage do not correspond to the expected time-bracket, what terminologies are to be adopted? And how such archaeological situations are to be interpreted? In my considered opinion in the twenty-first century the attention should be paid to finer details of chronology, reconstruction of the history of the main techno-cultural traits, and of course ultimately proper understanding of various cultures in totality.

References

ALLCHIN, B & R. ALLCHIN. 1982. The Rise of Civilization in India and Pakistan. Cambridge.

BOSE, N.K. *et al.* 1960. 'Palaeoliths from Monghyr district, Bihar'. Man in India. Vol. 40.No. 1: 68-75.

DE TERRA, H. & T.T. PATERSON. 1939. Studies on the Ice Age in India and Associated Human Cultures. Carnegie Institute of Washington Publications No. 499. Washington.

FOOTE, R.B. 1914. 'On the occurrence of Stone Implements in various parts of Madras and North Arcot District'. Journal of Literature and Science. Series III.

GAMBLE, C. & O. SOFFER (Eds). 1990. The World at 18.000 B.P. (Low Latitude). Vol. 2. London.

JAYASWAL, V. 1978. Palaeohistory of India (A study of the Prepared core technique). Agam Kala Prakashan. Delhi.

JAYASWAL, V. 1990. 'Hunter-gatherers of the terminal Pleistocene in Uttar Pradesh, India'. The World at 18.000 B.P. (Low Latitude). Vol. 2. Eds. C. Gamble & O. Soffer. London : 237-254.

JAYASWAL, V. 1997. 'An Archaeological Evidence for Tribal Tradition in Central India: A Case Study of Microliths'. Facets of Indian Civilization: Recent Perspectives (Essays in Honour of Prof. B.B. Lal).

Vol. I. (Ed. J.P. Joshi). Aryan Books International. New Delhi: 35-49.

JOSHI, R.V. 1978. Stone Age Cultures of Central India (Report on the Excavations of Rock-shelters at Adamgarh , Mdhya Pradesh). Poona.

LAL, B.B. 1958. 'Birbhanpur, a Microlithic Site in the Damodar Valley, West Bengal'. Ancient India. No. 14: 4-48.

MANOJ KUMAR. 2004. An Ethno-archaeological Study of Neolithic Cultures of Northern and Eastern India. (Unpublished) Ph.D. thesis, Banaras Hindu University. Varanasi.

MURTY, M.L.K. 1969. 'Blade and Burin Industries near Renigunta on the south-east coast of India'. Proceedings Prehistoric Society. Vol. XXXIV: 83-101.

NAGAJARA RAO, M.S. & K.C. MOHAPATRA. 1965. Stone Hill-dwellers of Tekkalkotta. Poona.

PADDAYYA, K. 1982. The Acheulian Culture of the Hunsgi Valley (Peninsular India): A Settlement System Perspective. Deccan College Postgraduate and Research Institute, Poona.

PANT, P.C. & V. JAYASWAL. 1977-78. 'Jamalpur : A Typological Variant within the Middle Palaeolithic Culture Complex of India'. Puratattva. Bulletin of Indian Archaeological Society. No. 9: 15-33.

PANT, P.C. & V. JAYASWAL. 1991. Paisra: The Stone Age Settlement of Bihar. Agam Kala Prakashan.

PANT, P.C. 1982. Prehistoric Uttar Pradesh (A Study of Old Stone Age). Delhi.

SANKALIA, H.D. 1962. Prehistory and Protohistory in India and Pakistan. Bombay.

SHARMA, A.K. 1991. "Neolithic Gufkral". Indian Archaeologial Heritage. New Delhi: 102-110.

SHARMA, G.R. & J.D.CLARK (Ed.). 1983. Palaeoenvironments and Prehistory in the Middle Son Valley, Madhya Pradesh. Allahabad.

SHARMA, G.R. 1973. "Stone Age in Vindhyas and the Ganga Valley". Radiocarbon and Indian Archaeology. D.P. Agrwal & A. Ghosh (Ed). Bombay: 106-110.

SHARMA, G.R. et al. 1980. From Hunting and Food Gathering to Domestication of Plants and Animals : Beginnings of Agriculture (Epi-Palaeolithic to Neolithic. Excavations at Chopani-Mando, Mahdaha and Mahgarha). Allahabad.

SINGH, B.P. 2004. Early Farming Communities of the Kaimur (Excavation at Senuwar 1986-87,89-90). Publication Scheme. Jaipur.

SMITH, V.A. 1906. "Pigmy Flints". Indian Antiquary. Vol. 35: 185-95.

THAPAR, B.K. 1965. 'Neoloithic Problem in India'. Indian Prehistory: 1964. (Eds.). V.N. Misra & Mate. Poona.

THAPAR, B.K. 1985. Recent Archaeological Discoveries in India. UNESCO. Japan.

ZUNEUR, F. 1950. Stone Age and Pleistocene chronology in Gujarat. Poona.

ON THE STATUS OF INDIAN HOMINOID AND HOMINID FOSSILS

A.R. SANKHYAN

Anthropological Survey of India, Indian Museum Campus, 27 Jawaharlal Nehru Road, Calcutta- 700016, India.
E-mail < sankhyan51@rediffmail.com> Tel: 91-033-22861733/ 91-033-2421-6767; Fax: 91-033-2286-1799.

Abstract: Palaeoanthropological researches in India came to a slow pace after 1980s when the palaeoanthropologists took the hominoid molecular evidence as sacrosanct and restricted the existence of the last common ancestor (LCA) of the great ape-hominid lineage, as well as that of the Homo sapiens to African continent. The consequence of the "molecular vision" was an assault on Ramapithecus and Sivapithecus as well as on the Asian Homo erectus, denying their contributions to the Plio-Pleistocene hominid and to the Homo sapiens ancestry, respectively. Despite of this, we still are away from identifying the anatomically appropriate Last Common Ancestor of the "African Ape-hominid" clade and are also unable to prevent the seekers of the "Multiregional Origins" of modern Homo sapiens in view of the wider distribution of the "archaic" Homo sapiens in the Old World. This communication comments on some of these points in the light of new fossil evidences, especially from South Asia.
The Central Narmada Valley has yielded a partial cranium and a few postcranial fossils of the middle Pleistocene hominin from Hathnora. The cranium was initially claimed to represent an "evolved" H. erectus, but subsequent and present re- inferred assessments suggest that it represents a large-headed / large-bodied unique species/clade of "archaic" Homo sapiens that could have been ancestral to both the H. sapiens and European pre-Neanderthals. The postcranial evidence apparently comes from a different very short and stocky robust built archaic hominin. Its body dimensions estimated from three postcranials- two clavicles and the ninth rib, yield estimates of 115 to 135 cm stature and 29-30 cm upper shoulder width, paralleling the Andaman Pygmy, and therefore reflect tropical adaptations to warm and humid climate.. The postcranial evidence therefore reveals the existence of Pygmy-sized early Homo sapiens in the middle Pleistocene of Narmada Valley-which might have served as the corridor for early human migrations across continents.
Keywords: Palaeoanthropology, hominid, origin, fossil, South Asia

Résumé: Les recherches paléoanthropologiques en Inde devinrent retardées après 1980, quand les paléoanthropologues ont pris les évidences moléculaires combo sacrosaintes et ont restreint l'existence du dernier ancêtre commun (LCA) du long lignage singe-hominide, ainsi que de l'Homo Sapiens, au continent Africain. La conséquence de la "vision moléculaire" fut un assaut au Ramapithecus et au Sivapithecus, ainsi qu'à l'Homo Erectus Asiatique, niant leurs contributions pour l'ancêtreté des hominidés du Plio-Pleistocène et de l'Homo Sapiens, respectivement. Malgré ceci, on est encore loin d'identifier le dernier ancêtre commun, anatomiquement approprié, du "Singe-Homme Africain" ainsi que d'éviter la quête des défenseurs des "Origines Multirégionales » de l'Homo Sapiens moderne, en vue de la distribution très large de l'Homo Sapiens "archaïque" dans le vieux Monde. Cette communication commente certains de ces points à la lumière de nouvelles évidences fossiles, spécialement de l'Asie du Sud.
La vallée centrale de Narmada a livré un crâne partial et quelques fossiles post-crâniens, de l'hominin du Pleistocène moyen de Hathora. Le crâne fut d'abord identifié comme représentatif d'un H. Erectus "évolué", mais après et à présent des approches sugèrent qu'il représente une variante unique, à large tête et corps, de l'Homo Sapiens "archaïque", lequel pourrai être un ancêtre soit de l'Homo Sapiens que des pré-Néandetaliens Européens. Les évidences post-craniales viennent, apparemment, d'un homini archaïque, très petit et robuste. Ses dimensions, calculées sur la base de trois os post-craniens – deux clavicules et la neuvième côte – sont estimées entre 115 et 125 cm de stature et 29.30 cm de largeur aux épaules, ressemblant au Piigmé de Andaman, et ainsi reflétant les adaptations tropicales a un climat chaux et humide. L'évidence post-craniale révèle ainsi l'existence d'un Homo Sapiens de taille pigmée, au Pleistocène moyen de la vallée de Narmada, lequel aurait pu servir de couloir pour les premières migrations humaines entre continents.
Mots clés: Paléoanthropologie, hominin, origine, fossile, Asie du Sud

INTRODUCTION

India has witnessed two major evolutionary events in the hominid prehistory. The first is witnessed in the Miocene sediments of the Siwalik Hills of Northwest sub-Himalayas, which preserves the evolutionary story of the hominoid radiation. The hominoid fossils from Siwaliks span a period of about six million years ranging from 12.3 to 5.0 mya with the late survival of "*Ramapithecus*" (Sankhyan, 1985). They form the ancestral substratum of the extant apes and probably that of the Plio-Pleistocene hominids as well in view of the molecular dates of the divergence of the extant ape and hominid lineages that has occurred sometimes during this period. After a substantial palaeontological hiatus between the last hominoid and the earliest *Homo,* the second evolutionary event recorded in Indian prehistory goes back to just unto the Middle Pleistocene- around half a million years ago. And, nowhere in South Asia other than the Central Narmada Valley has recorded this event through unequivocal fossil evidence, though some fossils from Siwaliks are claimed to be still older.

PART I: THE STATUS AND AFFINITIES OF INDIAN HOMINOIDS

The last two decades' great progress in molecular phylogenetics radically influenced our understanding of the fossil-based hominoid phylogeny, such that palaeo-anthropologists took the molecular evidence as sacrosanct believing that it presented a real branching pattern of the extant great apes and humans. Although, the traditional understanding of the fossils of Siwalik *Ramapithecus* or

African *Kenyapithecus* had suggested very early origins of the hominid lineage, but the Molecular Clock advocated a very late branching of the human and chimpanzee *(Pan)* lineages from a unique 'Last Common Ancestor' (LCA), while the Gorilla *(Gorilla)* and the Orangutan *(Pongo pygmaeus)* had splitted much earlier. The consequences were drastic. A major onslaught came on *Ramapithecus* and *Sivapithecus*, which were removed both from the Hominidae and were relegated to the "Pongidae" -thereafter restricted to *Pongo pygmaeus,* the lineage of the Orangutan. A partial cranium of *Sivapithecus* from Potwar Siwaliks (Pilbeam *et al.*, 1982) is taken as evidence for uniting *Sivapithecus* with the Orangutan whereas *Ramapithecus* was sunk into *Sivapithecus* on the basis of a shared dental dietary 'adaptive pattern' and allometry (Greenfield, 1979) and partly also for sexual dimorphism (Kelley & Pilbeam, 1986, Sankhyan, 1988b, 1991; etc.).

But, the removal of *Sivapithecus* / *Ramapithecus* had perplexing repercussions on the anatomical identity of the "chimpanzee-human" LCA. While Greenfield (1979, 1981) retained *Sivapithecus* / *Ramapithecus* as a 'generalized hominoid ancestor to the three great apes and humans, more palaeoanthropologists, notably Pilbeam *et al.* (1982) and Andrews (1982), viewed these exclusively on the Orangutan lineage, and their first appearance as the evidence of splitting of the lineage. Only a minority, e.g., Kay & Simons (1982) maintained the traditional hominid status even after accepting the merger of *Sivapithecus* and *Ramapithecus*. Another minority argued that *Sivapithecus* equally qualifies for the common ancestry of both Orangutan and Man (Schwartz, 1984; Sankhyan, 1988, 1990, 1998), though diametrically opposite to the popular molecular viewpoint.

How to identify the Great Ape-Human LCA?

General Hypothesis

The debate or controversy on the 'LCA' surfaces primarily due to a *priori* acceptance of the molecular phylogeny and re-interpretation of the fossil evidence fitting in the molecular frame. Although *Sivapithecus* and *Ramapithecus* have been dismissed from human ancestry, yet the "human-African ape" LCA is conceived to be "dentally *Sivapithecus*-like but cranio-facially Chimpanzee-hominid-like" (Lipson & Pilbeam, 1982; and many others). Among the *Sivapithecus* dental traits, the most important and commonly talked about is the thickness of the molar enamel, associated with the mandibular and maxillary robusticity, megadonty, etc. noted in hominids. Therefore, the basic assumption is that the thick enamel is a primitive retention (sympleisiomorphy) in the hominids-humans, whereas secondarily reduced or derived condition (Martin, 1985) in the African apes, owing to ecological shift for a soft / foliage/ frugivorous diet. Hence, the hominid-African ape cranio-facial similarities should be synapomorphies, inherited from their LCA. Historically, and apparently, the land of the 'Chimp-

human' LCA is Africa, which is undeniable because the earliest hominoids (*Proconsul* and other taxa) as well as the Plio-Pleistocene 'hominids' (including *Australopithecus, Paranthropus* and *Paranthropus*) come from Africa. This hard evidence coupled with the revelation of the 'molecular clock' spellbinds the palaeoanthropologists and molecular biologists to African continent, such that Europe and Asia are futile to hunt for the 'LCA'.

Which African/European Hominoid represents the LCA?

The 'molecular clock' based on albumins yield 0 – 4 million years dates for Chimpanzee-humans divergence. But, these are meaningless in view of the existence of australopithecines /paranthropines/ praeanthropines at 4-5 million years back. The same fate is of the better-claimed DNA – DNA hybridisation dates of 4 to 6 million years BP in consideration of 7-8 million years old fossils from Lothagam, Sumburu Hills conceived as the LCA. On the same consideration, the 6-7 million years old *Sahelanthropus tachadensis* from Chad cannot be designated as the LCA; it is also disputed as a unique chimpanzee or a female gorilla or even a hominid. The Sumburu Hill jaw possesses gorilla-like premolars and heavily enamelled molars with peg-like puffy appearance, and therefore unsuitable for the LCA. Hence, the African fossil evidence does not yet support the claim of "recent divergence".

Then, if we compromise with older divergence dates, the more appropriate candidate for the LCA could be *Kenyapithecus*. In 1970s, *Kenyapithecus* was also synonimised with *Ramapithecus* and later with *Sivapithecus*, but then resurrected in 1980s on consideration of anterior dental alignment, temporal and geographical gap between the two. Although, its post-canine morphology is inseparable from that of *Sivapithecus*, in enamel thickness it falls between *Afropithecus* and *Sivapithecus* (Leakey & Leaky, 1986). The cranio-facial morphology of *Kenyapithecus* is unknown, but both *Afropithecus* and *Sivapithecus* have aerorhynchous (upwardly turned) face. Post-cranially, *Kenyapithecus* presents a mosaic of primitive *Proconsul*-like and relatively derived *Dryopithecus* (=*Rudapithecus*)-like morphology, but does not resemble with any of the extant great apes. *D.* (=*Rudapithecus*) is, however, like *Sivapithecus* post-cranially. Thus, the available fossil evidence suggests *Kenyapithecus* as a primitive member of the Orangutan clade, lacking any affinity with the African apes, and these together with the hominids.

The above reveals that both on morphological and temporal considerations Africa have so far not yielded the purported 'Chimpanzee-hominid' LCA. Paradoxically, numerous fossil collecting from all over the Old world reveals a peculiar distribution pattern of the Late Miocene hominoids and Plio-Pleistocene hominids. While African continent shows a meagre yield of late Miocene hominoids between 13 to 7 mya- a period crucial for the existence of the 'LCA', both Asia and Europe have demonstrated rich occurrences and greater diversity of the hominoids during this time span. This, therefore, suggests that we may hunt for the 'Chimp-hominid' LCA outside Africa. Studies show frequent faunal exchanges between Africa and Eurasia during late Miocene.

As per the assumed character state polarity, the 'Chimp-hominid' LCA has to be thick-enamelled hominoid. The potential Eurasian taxa claimed by different authors include *Graecopithecus, Lufengpithecus,* Hungarian *Dryopithecus (= Rudapithecus)* and *Sivapithecus.*

The *Dryopithecus laietanus* from Spain (Moya-Sola & Kohler, 1996) placed the LCA of the three great apes just at 9.5 mya, which conflicts with other earlier claims based on the Hungarian *Dryopithecus* or the Greek hominoid, *Graecopithecus,* putting it at 12-13 million years ago. Further, the *Dryopithecus (D. laietanus)* is also claimed to be a primitive member of the great ape – human clade in the lack of a sub-arcuate fossa, robust zygomatics, the number and position of the zygomatico-maxillary for a-mina, and the temporal ridges bring *D. laietanus* to the Orangutan along with other hominoid taxa *Sivapithecus, Lufengpithecus,* and *Graecopithecus* as suggested by Schwartz (1990). *Dryopithecus* does not prove to be a unique last common ancestor of the African ape – human clade, but a primitive member of the Orangutan's clade, *Dryopithecus* now becomes a potential generalized late Miocene hominoid both dentally and postcranially from which both African as well as Asian great apes and Plio-Pleistocene hominids can be derived more parsimoniously.

Graecopithecus (=Ouranopithecus) was previously synonymies with *Sivapithecus* (Kay & Simons, 1983) on dental evidence. On the basis of a new cranio-facial as well as the traditional dental evidence, it has been claimed to be a unique late Miocene hominid ancestor. These characters include prominent glabellas, frontal sinus and brow ridges, broader intertribal distance, elongated nasoalveolar clivus ("African pattern"), molars squared, low-cusped and thick-enamelled, premolars molarized, canines reduced in size and the jaws robust and shallow ("sivapithecine dental pattern"). Though it is claimed to be male face, its reduced canine size is attributed to a female individual, questioning therefore its hominid status. Further, the similarities in the upper cranio-facial region of *Graecopithecus* are of primitive catarrhine in nature and that of the lower face (elongated premaxilla) including the brow ridge development are interpreted to be associated with the downward turning of the face with respect to the neuro-cranium (klinorhynchy), therefore, of low phtyletic valence. Andrews (1992) classified *Graeco-pithecus* in Homininae indet. However, an extremely klinorhynch face of the Greek specimen is more closely allied to the gorilla, but it cannot be regarded as an ancestor of gorilla without assumption of anatomical (dental) reversions. The phyletic status of *Graecopithe-cus,* therefore, remains outside the purview of the 'African ape – hominid' LCA.

There was also a claim of the LCA on the thin-enamelled Hungarian *Dryopithecus (= Rudapithecus).* It was based

mainly on the anterior dental and cranio-facial resemblances with the African apes, especially *Gorilla,* and *Australopithecus,* and so Begun (1992) speculated that the hominids shared a unique late common ancestor with the chimpanzee as the two have similarly elongated premaxillae and incisor morphology. But, these are likely convergences since there is considerable variation in the components of the premaxillary subnasal region in the extant and extinct hominoids and hominids and early men. This region of the face is important in sorting out different species and sub-species of the closely related taxa. The polarity of the subnasal and other facial similarities among distantly related taxa (such as differ in basic dental gnathic dietary adaptations) of the hominoids and hominids is always in doubt. Kay & Simons (1983) and Dean & Delson (1992) may be correct in interpreting *Pan-Australopithecus* premaxillary similarities as convergent or parallel developments, and the same is true for *Pan-Pongo* similarities.

Which Asian Hominoid represents the LCA?

After failing in search in Africa and Europe we may look into the Asian Late Miocene hominoids. The Chinese *Lufengpithecus* was earlier known as *Ramapithecus* and *Sivapithecus,* subsequently lumped together in Sivapi-thecus on dental criteria but later treated as a single highly sexually dimorphic species different at generic level in facial and palatal morphology. A subsequent detailed phylogenetic analysis of *Lufengpithecus* puts it next to *Sivapithecus* in the Orangutan clade, followed by *Graeco-pithecus* and *Rudapithecus* in the same broad clade by the synapomorphies of a superiorly expanded maxillary sinus, and lack of a supraorbital sulcus (except in *Graeco-pithecus).* No characteristics 'African' subnasal pattern is shown by *Lufengpithecus* but it shows rather 'Asian pattern', and likely a primitive catarrhine and placed this genus outside the mainstream of the Hominidae.

Involving parallel evolution of hominoid enamel thick-ness makes little sense when this trait occurs restrictedly among hominids as well among some taxa falling in the orangutan clade. A rather more straight and parsimonious explanation of thick enamel among hominids and the orangutans would be that both inherited this trait from a thick-enamelled common ancestor, and on the same logic the African apes inherited their thin enamel from a thin-enamelled (like dryopithecine) ancestor. The enamel thickness is therefore a relatively conservative trait and the dental-gnathic apparatuses with 'thin' or 'thick' (also includes intermediate thickness) enamel reflect diagonally opposite dietary adaptations of two types of hominoids, and their separate dietary adaptations of two types of hominoids and their separate dietary regimes, home ranges or dispersal pattern in different ecological systems. The thick-enamelled masti-catory apparatus of the *Sivapithecus* had been a positive advantageous selection for consuming a wider range of diet including hard stuffs available mainly in terrestrial and semi arboreal niches. This is probably why the thick-enamelled hominoids were

15

widespread during late Miocene and constituted an ancestral stock for hominids and orangutans. On the other hand, the thin-enamelled (dryopithecine) dental-gnathic apparatus in the African apes adapted to soft fruit or foliage diet of the tropical forest is of relative less selective advantage. This also explains why such hominoids were of limited occurrence during late Miocene and extremely rare during the latest Miocene to Pleistocene (as no evidence is as yet recovered) when woodland/savannah habitats and drier and colder conditions set in. This is also probably, why the immediate ancestors of the African apes are still unknown. Dental and gnathic characters are better sorters of the Miocene hominoid lineages than are the cranio-facial characters. The latter constitute a mixture of primitive and parallel/convergent similarities. A number of these characters could be related to airorhynchy in orangutan and siamang, and to a larger degree in the gibbons.

And African pygmy chimpanzee to moderate or low degree that is also seen in *Sivapithecus* and *Afropithecus* or related to klinorhynchy – in extreme from is African apes and *Graecopithecus* and to moderate degree in *Australopithecus*. The extant of these situations depends on the position of gravity while balancing the body and the facial loading on appendicular base in different arboreal or terrestrial postural or locomotory modes. As such, the characters linked with airorhynchy or klinorhynchy have little valence when we compare otherwise dentally different hominoids and hominids. These are more useful when taxa or species on a given lineage are compared.

Then what is the solution?

Since the "Chimp-hominid" LCA still not supported by the fossil evidence, *Sivapithecus* and *Ramapithecus* still remain open for debate. If we re-look on *Sivapithecus* partial skull from Potwar Siwaliks (Pilbeam *et al.*, 1982), we notice a mosaic of both 'hominid' (in the lower face) and 'pongid' (in the mid-face) characters. To be more specific, the characters of the lower face, i.e., the maxilla and mandible including the dentition, are quite hominid-like as observed in *Ramapithecus,* viz. megadont cheek teeth, the molars squared, low-cusped and thick-enamelled, the lower third premolars molarized with metaconid development, transverse orientation of the maxillary canines, relatively reduced canines, and shallow and robust mandibular rami and symphyses with strong external buttresses. Collectively, these features are referred to as "sivapithecine / "Asian dental pattern". The mid-face on the other hand, resembles that of the Orangutan in having: 'a narrow inter-orbital distance, tall orbits, prominent brow ridges and glabellar eminences, robust and flaring zygomatics, smooth nasal entrance, the arched and overlapping almost equally thickened hard palate and alveolar process resulting in a narrow incisive canal (see Lipson & Pilbeam, 1982; McCollum *et al.,* 1993). The large Turkey species of *Sivapithecus, S. meteai,* also resembles Orangutan in some of these features (Andrews & Tekkaya, 1980). Should then we regard *Sivapithecus* (including *Ramapithecus*)- a 'hominid' or a 'pongid' or both- common ancestor of hominids and pongids? If both, then the LCA was "dentally *Sivapithecus* and hominid like but craniofacially Orangutan-like". The lumping of *Sivapithecus-Ramapithecus* simply reveals a common ancestry of the hominids and the Orangutans, of course a diametrically opposite view unpalatable to a majority seeking African origins. As pointed out earlier, if the dental-gnathic similarities in *Sivapithecus-Pongo – Australopithecus* could evolve parallely, the mid-facial/premaxillary similarities in *Pan-Australopithecus* could be convergent or parallel developments. Hence, if re-interpreted, the first appearance of *Sivapithecus* in the Siwaliks at 12.3 million years ago denotes the splitting time of the hominid and Orangutan lineages.

Then Why a Conflict with the Molecular Clock?

Ruta and Coates (2003:224) maintain that the "fossils and molecules should be treated as complementary approaches rather than as conflicting and irreconcilable methods". But, Rodriguez-Trelles *et al.* (2003:5-6) are categorical in questioning the neutrality and therefore the reliability of the molecular Clock over time. Through their study of nine proteins they observed: "The hypothesis of the molecular clock was advanced on the grounds that most amino acid substitutions in a protein (or nucleotides in a gene) occur between functionally equivalent residues, so that their replacement along evolving lineages would be determined by mutation rate and time elapsed, rather than by natural selection.... Natural selection is rather fickle, subject to the vagaries of environmental change and organism interactions, whereas mutation rate for a given gene is likely to remain constant through time and across lineages. The number of amino acid replacements (or nucleotide substitutions) between species would, then, reflect the time elapsed since their last common ancestor. The time of remote events, as well as the degree of relationship among contemporary lineages could, thus be determined on the basis of amino acid (or nucleotide) differences. A notable feature of the hypothesis of the molecular evolutionary clock is multiplicity: every one of the thousands of proteins or genes of an organism is an independent clock, each ticking at a different rate but all measuring the same events (Ayala 1986; Gillespie 1991; Li 1997)".

However, Donoghue and Smith (2003: 3) conclude that the molecular clock estimate, palaeontological clock estimate and attempts to correlate the two are all hostage to a geological timescale that is under continual revision, thus, the choice of timescale is non-trivial... Unless all of these sources of error are taken into account, in addition to attempts to correlate fossils occurrences to the geological timescale, and those errors attendant to molecular clock themselves, errors will propagate, potentially beyond the age of the events be estimated".

Concluding Remarks

Are morphology and the molecules in conflict? Are their polarities the same to expect a compromise? There are obvious fundamental differences in the scale of evolution that occurs at morphological (or gross/macro level) and at molecular (micro/biochemical level) as the adaptive mechanisms in the two are different and ought to follow different rate or even opposite courses, such that the morphological and molecular affinities may not convey the same meaning or polarity. Hence, there should not be a surprise if we observe a conflict in drawing a phyological inference from the two altogether different sets of data. But, Andrews & Martin (1987: 113) were surprised as they observed: "the only real surprises are that the clear shared derived similarities at the molecular level among the African apes and humans are not strongly reflected in the morphological analysis and that the morphological similarities between African apes are not reflected at the molecular level". On such a situation many scholars still maintain that the *Homo-Pan-Gorilla* triad remains unresolved (Groves & Paterson, 1991). But, the obvious reason for this paradox is that the polarity of the morphological and molecular homologies is at the opposite poles, i.e., if one set were 'shared-derived', the other set could have been 'shared-primitive'.

Human African ape molecular similarities are regarded as 'shared-derived' on the notion that lesser the time elapsed after divergence from the LCA, the more similar are the descendents, and the *vice versa*, assuming uniform rates of molecular changes in all hominoid lineages (called "rate test"). This could hold good when broad anthropoid/ radiations are compared, viz., Cercopithecoidea, Ceboidea and Hominoidea. But, within the Hominoidea, where the molecular differences are less sharp, true/correct picture of hominoid cladogenesis may not be obtained, because of (as many notable molecular biologists have observed) extremely slow rate of molecular evolution in the human and African apes, especially the chimpanzee, while hominid morphological evolution occurred very rapidly. This made the difference in the polarity. Therefore, the *Homo-Pan/Gorilla* molecular similarities may necessarily not be the late synapomorphies, but retention of early symplesiomophies of the common hominoid ancestor, before the split of the orangutan lineage that independently accumulated their morphological and molecular differences. Although, it is not easy to change the popular stand, yet if we are prepared to accept this interpretation, we will find no conflict between morphology and the molecule.

THE STATUS AND AFFINITIES OF INDIAN HOMINIDS

The recent molecular/DNA evidence has also influenced the interpretation of the hominid/hominin fossils. This directly or indirectly follows the "Punctuated Equi-

librium" model adhering to the "African or Single Origin" or "African Eve" hypothesis. These follow 'Cladistics' for understanding the character state polarity, which heavily relies upon a few novel synapomorphies (shared derived characters) to support a recent common ancestry. But, there are still followers of the 'Darwinian Gradualism' is not threatened by the doctrine of 'Punctuated Equilibrium', who believe that the relationships among the fossil species that experienced a long and episodic evolutionary past through the operation of natural selection and other evolutionary forces are better explained by the 'grade' concept. However, both 'grade' and 'clade' concepts are helpful in generating different and meaningful scenarios.

The status of the fossil Indian hominids, has also invited similar debate on cladistic and gradistic interpretations. As on record now we have two types of hominids (preferred to be called as hominins) from Narmada Valley documented. While the one is represented by the partial Skullcap- the right Calvarium (Sonakia, 1984) and the other by three postcranial bones- two clavicles and a 9th rib (Sankhyan, 1997a&b, 2005).

The Phyletic Status of the 'Large' Hominin: The Cranial Evidence

Represented by the partial Skullcap (Calvarium), the hominin was initially argued belonging to the so-called "evolved" *Homo erectus* (Lumley and Sonakia, 1985b; Sonakia, 1999, 2005). But subsequently, the cladistic view found more acceptances designating it belonging to the so-called "archaic" *Homo sapiens* (e.g., Kennedy *et al.*, 1991, Kennedy, 1992, 1999, 2000, 2005). Cameron *et al.* (2004) have also joined the cladistic group with the difference they specified its European ancestry shared with the Neandertals or pre-Neandertals, in particular with the Steinheim man (also an "archaic" *Homo sapiens*), migrant to South Asia earlier to 250 ka. The Narmada calvarium is also assigned to *H. heidelbergensis* (Rightmire, 1988), a supposedly widely occurring Middle –Late Pleistocene species that is believed to have ruled Europe and Africa, and probably East Asia as well. The Narmada calvarium thus drags into the historical debate between the 'Multi-regional' vs. 'Single Origins' hypotheses, dealt with the author elsewhere (Sankhyan, 1999). The usages of "evolved" or "archaic" are redundant with the current cladistic phylogenetics, and so generally not acceptable to a majority of the scholars.

However, based on his own observations on the calvarium, the author (Sankhyan, 2005) observed relative degree of relatedness in 26 mensural traits in the decreasing order is as follows: the Petralona (11)> La Ferrassie (10)> the La Chapelle Aux Saint (8)> the Kabwe / Dali/ Zkd 10 / Ngadong11/ Sangiran 17 (7)> the Ceprano and Steinheim (6)> the Arago/ Saccapastor/ Amud / Sambrumenchan (5)> Shanidar1 / Mt Carmel (4)> ER3733 / OH9/ Zkd11, 12 / Swascombe / Ehrndorf (3)> Skhul (2)> Cro-Magnon (1).

The La Ferrassie and the La Chapelle Aux Saintare are well known classical Neanderthals restricted in distribution to Europe. Martinez & Arsuaga, (1997) have also classified the Petralona and other European "archaic" *H. sapiens* under Neanderthals with restricted occurrences and local evolution in Europe. On this consideration, the author is inclined to view the hominin as quite "unique", with only the generalized affinities to the Euroasian middle to late Pleistocene hominins. As such cladistically, it may be more befitting to regard the Calvarium forming a different clade of a stem hominin ancestral to both *H. sapiens* and Neanderthals. If so, it may merit a new *nomen* of *H. narmadensis*.

The Phyletic Status of the 'Small' Hominin: The Post-Cranial Evidence

Earlier, the author (Sankhyan, 1999) had argued that the Narmada hominin fossil cranial and postcranial elements might belong to a single 'unusual individual' -with large head on a dwarf body- on the grounds that the anatomical elements are sexed as female, are of similar inferred age (about 30 years) of at death, shared the same stratigraphic level, and found close by. But, these arguments could generate more opposition from the peers, such that the alternatively argument was advanced (Sankhyan, 2006) that the large cranium does not scale with the very short clavicles and the rib, such that we have encountered two different types of hominins co-existing in the Central Narmada Valley.

As hinted by the author earlier (Sankhyan, 1997, 2005), a recent detailed comparative morphometric statistical analysis by him (Sankhyan, in Press), the clavicles present a very robust but uniquely short and stocky hominin, likely not exceeding 133 cm in stature. The estimates of the upper chest width-i.e., the horizontal breadth across the shoulders from the two clavicles are very important findings. These are 29-30 cm and fall at the mean value of 30 cm of the Greater Andamanese and the Onges of the Little Andaman. The estimated stature as well as the upper chest width both is on the scale of the shortest extant Pygmy female, and obviously different from the tall and broad-chested Neanderthals and other Europian "archaic" *Homo sapiens* including African early *Homo erectus* or *H. ergaster*. Another important finding is that the clavicle shows mesocleidic condition (modern rounding of the diaphysis)- which is a derived evolutionnary advancement of modern *Homo sapiens,* suggesting that the 'small' Narmada *Homo* had entered into the 'sapiensdom', despite of retention of many *Homo erectus* primitive pleisiomorphies.

It is understandable that the 'large' and 'small' hominins at Hathnora come from two different breeding isolates, and not from two different species, since sympatric co-existence of two species is not seen in humans. Even the Pygmy occupies a separate ecological niche as they at different cultural levels than the dominant large-sized humans. A large collection of the Palaeolithic implements from Hathnora is presently under study, yet it we visualise an inter-phase of the Late Acheulian and Middle Palaeolithic cultures (Sankhyan, 1997b); Lumley & Sonakia (1985a), Badam *et al.* (1986) and Bhattacharya & Sonakia (1989) also reported Late Acheulian tools. These may favour younger dates but certainly much older than 75 kya based on the YTA- "Youngest Toba Ash" datum (Chesner et al., 1991; Acharyya and Basu, 1993) based . The Early Acheulian dated at Bori at c. 670 kya (Misra, *et al.,* 1995) may be used as the lower datum for Narmada Lower Palaeolithic; further greater antiquity claimed by some geologists is restricted by the palaeomagnetic reversal c. 730 kya at Dhansi (Rao *et al.,* 1997; Agrawal *et al.,* 1988), underlying unconformably by the Hathnora "Boulder Conglomerate" (strictly speaking cemented Pebble Conglomerate) of the Surajkund Formation (Tiwari & Bhai, 1997), bearing the human fossils. The palaeontologists speak for middle Pleistocene (c. 500 kya) on bio-stratigraphy (Biswas, 1997). On the whole, we may restrict the antiquity of Hathnora between c. 200 and 500 kya.

Based on the present human and diverse faunal fossils in situ with innumerable Palaeolithic implements, the author (Sankhyan, 1999) has viewed Central Narmada Valley as a Pleistocene haven and refuge when severe climatic conditions prevailed in the northern part of the subcontinent. Narmada valley is also important as it occupies a strategic mid-continental place between South-East Asia and West Asia, and therefore, might have served as one of the east-west passages to the prehistoric populations across Asia and Africa. It is now fairly clear that the valley was a meeting place for diverse human ethnic and cultural elements since the Palaeolithic times as has been documented by different Stone Age industries and the prehistoric rock-paintings, for instance the famous Bhimbetka, Adamgarh, Nakti Talai, Pachmarhi, etc. preserved in numerous rock shelters of the Satpura and Vindhyan hills, confining the valley, lead the author to regard central Narmada valley as the "paradise" of the Prehistoric man in South Asia.

Acknowledgements

The author acknowledges the encouragements and academic provided by Dr. V.R. Rao, the present Director Anthropological Survey of India.

References

I. On Hominoids:

ANDREWS, P. 1985. Family group systematics and evolution among catarrhine primates. In *Ancestors: The Hard Evidence.* E, Delson (ed.) New York: Alan R. Liss, pp. 14-22.

ANDREWS, P. 1986. The molecular evidence for catarrhine evolution. In *Major Topics in Primate and*

Human Evolution. B. Wood, L. Martin and P. Andrews (eds.) Cambridge: Cambridge University Press, pp. 107-129.

ANDREWS, P. 1987. Aspects of hominoid phylogeny. In *Molecules and Morphology in Evolution: Conflict or Compromise?* C Patterson (des). Cambridge: Cambridge University Press, pp. 23-53.

ANDREWS, P. 1990. Lining up the ancestors. *Nature* 345: 664-665.

ANDREWS, P. and J.E. CRONIN, 1982. The relationships of *Sivapithecus* and *Ramapithecus* and the evolution of Orang-Utan. *Nature* 297: 541-546.

ANDREWS, P. and L. MARTIN, 1987. Cladistic relationships of extant and fossil hominoids. J. Human Evolution. 16: 101-118.

ANDREWS, P. and L. TEKKAYA, 1980. A revision of Turkish Miocene hominoid Sivapithecus metai. Paleontology 23: 85-95.

BENVENISTE, R.E. and G.J. TODARO, 1976, evolution of type C viral genes: Evidence for an Asian origin of Man. *Nature* 261: 101-108.

BERNOR, R.L. 1983. Geochronology and zoogeographic relationships of Miocene Hominoidea. *In New Interpretations of Ape and Human Ancestry, R.L.* R.L. Ciochon and R.S. Corruccini (eds.). New York: Plenum Press, pp. 21-64.

BOAZ, N.T. 1983. Morphological trends and phylogenetic relationships from middle Miocene hominoids to late Pliocene hominids. *In New Interpretations of Ape and Human Ancestry.* R.L. Ciochon, and R.S. Corruccini (eds.). New York: Plenum Press, pp. 705-720.

CHOPRA, S.R.K., S. KAUL and R. PATHAK, 1982. Morphometric affinities in innominate bones of Old World primates including Man. *J. Human Evolution 11: 105-108.*

CIOCHON, R.L. and R.S. CORRUCCINI, 1983. *New Interpretations of Ape and Human Ancestry,* New York: Plenum Press.

CONSTANS, J., C. GOUAILLARD, C. BOUISSOU and J.M. DUGOUJON, 1987. Polymorphism of the Vitamine D binding protein (DBP) among primates: An evolutionary analysis. *Am. J. Phys. Anthrop.* 73: 365-377.

DE BONIS, L., 1983. Phyletic relationships of Miocene hominoids and higher primate classification. *In New Interpretations of Ape and Human ancestry.* R.L. Ciochon and R.S. Corruccini (eds.). New York: Plenum Press, pp. 625-649.

DE BONIS, L., G. BOUVRAIN, P. GERAADS and G. KOUFOS, 1990. New hominoid skull material from the late Miocene of Macedonia in Northern Greece. *Nature 345: 712-714.*

DELSON, E. 1985. Catarrhine evolution. In *Ancestors, The Hard evidence.* E. Delson (ed.) New York: Alan R. Liss, pp 9-13. – 1985. The earliest *Sivapithecus. Nature* 318: 107-108.

GANTT, D. G. 1983. The enamel of Neogene hominoids: Structural and Phyletic implications. In *New interpretations of ape and human Ancestry.* R.L. Ciochon and R.S. Corruccini (eds.). New York: Plenum Press, pp. 249-298.

GINGERICH, P.D. 1985. Nonlinear Molecular Clocks and Ape-Human divergence times. In *Hominoid Evolution: Past, Present and Future. P.V. Tobias (ed.). New York: Alan R. Liss, pp. 411-416.*

GOODMAN, M. 1976. Towards a genealogical classifycation of the primates. In *Molecular Anthropology.* M. Goodman and R.E. Tashian (eds.). New York: Plenum Press, pp. 321-264.

GOODMAN, M. 1982, Bimolecular evidence on human origins from the standpoint of Darwinian theory. *Human Biology* 54: 247-264.

GOODMAN, M. 1989. Update to "Evolution of the immunologic species specificity of human serum proteins". *Human Biology* 61: 925-934.

GOODMAN, M. and R.E. TASHIAN, 1976. *Molecular Anthropology.* New York: Plenum Press.

GOODMAN, M., M.L. BABA and L.L. DARGA, 1983. The bearing of molecular data on the cladogenesis and times of divergence of hominoid lineages. In *New Interpretations of Ape and Human Ancestry.* R. L. Ciochon and R.S. Corruccini (eds.). New York: Plenum Press, p. 67-86.

GREENGIELD, L.O. 1979. On the adaptive pattern of "Ramapithecus". *Am. J. Phys. Anthrop.* 50: 527-548.

GREENGIELD, L.O. 1980. A late divergence hypothesis. *Am. J. Phys. Anthrop.* 52: 351-365.

GREENGIELD, L.O. 1983. Towards resolution of discrepancies between phenetic and palaeontological data bearing on the question of human origins. In *New Interpretations of Ape and Human Ancestry.* R.L. Ciochon and R.S. Corruccini (eds.). New York: Plenum Press. Pp. 695-703.

HARTMAN, S. E. 1988. A cladistic analysis of hominoid molars. *J. Human Evolution* 17: 489-502.

KAY, R.F. 1981. The nut-crackers: A new theory of the adaptations of the Ramapithecinae. *Am. J. Phys. Anthrop.* 55: 143-151.

KAY, R. F. and E. L. SIMONS, 1983. A reassessment of the relationship between later Miocene and subsequent hominoids. In *New Interpretations of Ape and Human Ancestry.* R. L. Ciochon and R. S. Corruccini (eds.). New York: Plenum Press. Pp. 577-624.

KELLEY, J. and D. PILBEAM, 1986. The Dryopithecines: Taxonomy, comparative anatomy and phylogeny of Miocene large hominoids. In *Comparative Primate Biology. Vol. I: Systematics. Evolution, and Anatomy.* D. Swindler and J. Erwin (eds.).: New York. Alan R. Liss. Pp. 61-411.

KOOP, B.R., M. GOODMAN, P. ZU, K. CHAN and J.L. SLINGHTON, 1986. Primate n-globin DNA segments and man's place among the great apes. *Nature* 319: 234-238.

LEAKEY, R.E. and M.G. LEAKEY, 1986. A new Miocene hominoid from Kenya. *Nature* 324: 146-148.

LIPSON, S. and D. PILBEAM, 1982. Ramapithecus and hominoid evolution. *J. Human Evolution* 11: 343-348.

LI, W.H. and M. TANIMURA, 1987. The molecular clock runs more slowly in man than in apes and monkeys. *Nature* 326: 93-96.

MAI, L.L. 1983. A model of the chromosome evolution and its bearing on cladogenesis in the Hominoidea. In new Interpretations of Ape and Human Ancestry. R. L. Ciochon and R.S. Corruccini (eds.). New York: Plenum Press, pp. 87- 114.

MARTIN, L. 1985. Significance of enamel thickness in hominoid evolution. *Nature* 314: 260-263.

MARTIN, L. 1986. Relationships among extant and extinct great apes and humans. In *Major tropics in Primate and human Evolution*. B. Wood, L. Martin and P. Andrews (eds.). Cambridge: Cambridge University Pres, pp, 161-187.

MARTIN, L. 1986. A book review of: *New Interpretations of Ape and Human Ancestry*. R. L. Ciochon and R.S. Corrucinnin (eds.). J. Human Evolution. 15: 219-221.

MARTIN, R.D. 1990. *Primate Origins and Evolution: A Phylogenetic Reconstruction*. London: Chapman and Hill.

OXNARD, C.E. 1975. The place of the Australopithecines in human evolution: Grounds for doubt? *Nature* 258: 389-395.

OXNARD, C.E. 1977. Morphometric affinities of the human shoulder. *Am. J. Phys. Anthrop.* 46: 367-374.

OXNARD, C.E. 1984. *The order of the Man*. London: New Heaven.

OXNARD, C.E. 1987. *Fossil, Teeth and Sex: Perspectives on Human evolution*. Washington: Hong Kong University Press.

PICKFORD, M. 1983. Sequence and environments of the lower and Middle Miocene hominoids of western Kenya. In *New Interpretations of Ape and Human Ancestry*. R.L. Ciochon and R.S. Corruccini (eds.). New York: Plenum Press. Pp. 411-439.

PICKFORD, M. 1985. A new look at Kenyapithecus based on recent discoveries in western Kenya. *J. Human Evolution* 14: 113-143.

PILBEAM, D. 1985. Patterns of hominoid evolution. In *Ancestors: The Hard Evidence*. E. Delson (ed.). New York: Alan R. Liss, pp. 51-59.

PILBEAM, D. 1986. Distinguished Lecture: Hominoid evolution and hominoid origins. *Am. Anthropologist* 88: 295-312.

PILBEAM, D. and L.L. JACOBS, 1978. Changing views on human origins. *Plateau* 51: 18-30.

PILBEAM, D., M.D. ROSE, C. BADGLEY and B. LIPSCHUTZ, 1980. Miocene hominoids from Pakistan. *Postilla* 188: 1-95.

PILBEAM, D., M.D. ROSE, J.C. BARRY and S.M.I. SHAT, 1990. New Sivapithecus humari from Pakistan and the relationship of Sivapithecus and Pongo. *Nature* 348: 237- 239.

PROST, J. 1980. The origin of bipedalism. *Am. J. Phys. Anthrop.* 52: 175-190.

RAZA, S.M., J.C. BARRY, D. PILBEAM, M.D. ROSE, S.M.I. SHAH and S. WARD, 1983. New hominoid primates from the middle Miocene Chinji Formation, Potwar Plateau, Pakistan. *Nature* 305: 52-54.

RODMAN, P.S. and H.M. MCHENRY, 1980. Bioenergetics and the origin of hominoid bipedalism. *Am. J. Phys. Anthrop.* 52: 103-106.

ROMERO-HERERA, A.E., H. LEHMAN, K.A. JOYSEY and A.E. FRIDAY, 1976. Evolution of myoglobin amino acid sequences in primates and other vertebrates. In *Molecular Anthropology*. M. Goodman and R.E.Tashian (eds.). New York: Plenum Press, pp. 289-300.

ROSE, M.D. 1983. Miocene hominoid postcranial morphology monkey-like, ape-like, or both? In *New Interpretations of Ape and Human Ancestry*. R. L. Ciochon and R.S. Corruccini (eds.). New York: Plenum Press, pp. 405-417.

ROSE, M.D. 1984. Hominoid postcranial specimens from the middle Miocene Chinji Formation, Pakistan. *J. Human Evolution* 13: 503-516.

ROSE, M.D. 1986, Further hominoid postcranial specimens from the late Miocene Nagri Formation of Pakistan. *J. Human Evolution* 15. 333-367.

SANKHYAN, A.R. 1984. An Orangutan Hypothesis: A solution to palaeontological and molecular controversy on Ape/Man ancestry and divergence. *Manuscript*.

SANKHYAN, A.R. 1985. Man shared a late common ancestry with the Asian orangutan but not with the African chimpanzee or gorilla. Paper presented at the Anthropology and Archaeology Section. *72nd Session, Indian Science Congress*, Lucknow, Jan. 1985.

SANKHYAN, A.R. 1985. Late occurrence of Sivapithecus in Indian Siwaliks. *J. Human Evolution* 14: 573-578.

SANKHYAN, A.R. 1986. A fresh look on the Miocene hominoids and the problem of last common ancestry. Paper presented at the *Anthropology and Archaeology Section, 73rd Session, Indian Science Congress*, Delhi, Jan., 1986.

SANKHYAN, A.R. 1986. Hominoid divergence: An overview and re-assessment of the stratophenetic evidence. Paper presented at the *UGC Seminar on Anthropology in India: Problems and Prospects,* Punjab University, Chandigarh, March, 1986.

SANKHYAN, A.R. 1988. On human ancestry: A new perspective. In *Current Anthropological and Archaeological Perspectives.* K.L. Bhowmik (ed.), Vol.-I, Man. New Delhi: Inter-India Publication, pp. 57-88.

SANKHYAN, A.R. 1990. An anthropological look on *Ramapithecus and Sivapithecus* Siwaliks hominoids. J. Himalayan Geology (In Press).

SARICH, V.M. and J.E. CRONIN, 1976. Molecular systematics of the primates. In *Molecular Anthropology.* M. Goodman and R.E. Tashian (eds.). New York: Plenum Press, pp. 141-170.

SCHWARTZ, J.H. 1984. The evolutionary relationships of human and orangutans. *Nature* 308: 501-505.

SCHWARTZ, J.H. 1984. Hominoid evolution: A review and reassessment. *Current Anthropology* 25: 655-672.

SCHWARTZ, J.H. 1987. *The Red Ape.* Boston: Houghton Mifflin Co.

SCHWARTZ, J.H. 1990. Lufengpithecus and its potential relationship to an orangutan clad. *J. Human Evolution* 19: 591-605.

SCHULTZ, A.H., 1986. The recent primates. In *Perspectives on Human Evolution.* S.L. Washburn and P.C.Jay (eds.) New York: Holt Renehart and Winston, pp. 122-195.

SIBLEY, C.G. and J.E. AHLIZUIST, 1984. The phylogeny of the hominoid primates as indicated by DNA-DNA hybridization. *J. Molecular Evolution*: 371-389.

SIMONS, E.L. and D.R. PILBEAM, 1965. Preliminary revision of Dryopithecines (Pongidae, Anthropoidea). Folia Primatologica 3: 81-152.

SIMONS, E.L. and D.R. PILBEAM, 1972. Hominoid palaeoprimatology. In *The Functional and Evolutionary Biology of Primates.* R.H. Tuttle (ed.). Aldine: Atherton, pp. 36-70.

STANYON, R. and B. CHIARELLI, 1982 Phylogeny of the Hominoidea: The chromosomal evidence. *J. Human Evolution* 11: 493-504.

SWARTS, J.D. 1988. Deciduous dentition: Implication for hominoid phylogeny. In *Orangutan Biology.* J.H. Schwartz (ed.) Oxford: Oxford University Press, pp. 263-282.

TUTTLE, R. and G.W. CORTRIGHT, 1988. Positional behavior, adaptive complexes, and evolution. In *Orangutan Biology.* J. H. Schwartz (ed.). New York: Oxford University Press, pp. 311-330.

VRBA, E.S. 1979. A new study of the scapula of Australopithecus. Am. J. Phys. Anthrop. 51: 117-130.

WARD, S.C. and D. PILBEAM, 1983. Maxillo-facial morphology of Miocene hominoids from Africa and Indo-Pakistan. In *New Interpretations of Ape and Human ancestry.* R. L. Ciochon and R.S. Corruccini (eds.) New York: Plenum, pp. 211-238.

WARD, S.C. and W.H. KIMBEL, 1983. Subnasal alveolar morphology and the systematic position of Sivapithecus. *Am. J. Phys. Anthrop.* 61: 157-171.

WOLPOFF, M. H. 1982. Ramapithecus and hominid origins. *Current Anthropology* 23: 501-522.

WU, R. 1987. a REVISION OF THE CLASSIFICATION OF THE Lufeng great apes. Acta Anthrop. *Sinica* 6: 265-271.

YAMAZAKI, N. and H. ISHIDA, 1984. A biomechanical study of the vertical climbing and bipedal walking in gibbons. *J. Human Evolution* 13: 563-571.

ZIHLAMAN, A.L. and J.M. LOWENSTEIN, 1983. Ramapithecus and Pan paniscus: Significance for human origins. In New Interpretations of Ape and human ancestry. R.L. Ciochon and R.S. Corruccini (eds.) New York: Plenum, pp. 677-698.

ZUCKERKANDL, E. 1976. Programmes of gene action and progressive evolution. In *Molecular Anthropology.* M. Goodman and E.E. Tashian (eds.). New York: Plenum, pp. 387-447.

II. On Hominids:

ACHARYYA, S.K. and BASU, P.K., 1993. Toba Ash on the Indian subcontinent and its implications for the correlation of Late Pleistocene Alluvium. Quat. Research 40, 10-19.

AGRAWAL, D.P., KOTLIA, B.S. and KUSUMGAR, S., 1988. Chronology and significance of the Narmada Formations. Proc. Ind. Nat. Sci. Acad. 54A, 418-424.

BADAM, G.L., GANJOO, R.K., SALAHUDDIN, R.K.G. and RAJAGURU, S.N., 1986. Evolution of fossil hominin – the maker of Late Acheulean tools at Hathnora, Madhya Pradesh, India. Curr. Sci. 55 (3), 143-145.

BADAM, G.L., 2001. Palaeontological excavations in Narsinghpur Distt., Central Narmada valley, Madhya Pradesh, India. Puratan 12, 61-76.

BHATTACHARYA, D.K. and SONAKIA, A., 1989. Cultural remains from the earliest hominin site on Narmada. In: Tiwari, S.C. (ed.), Changing Perspectives of Anthropology in India. Today and Tomorrow's Printers and Publishers, New Delhi, pp. 313-320.

BISWAS, B., 1997. Fossil mammalia of the Quaternary sequence of the Narmada Valley: Their affinity, age and ecology. In: Quaternary Geology of the Narmada Valley, Geol. Surv.Ind., Calcutta, Spl. Publn. No. 46, pp 91-104.

BROWN, P., SUTIKNA, T., MORWOOD, M.J., SOEJONO, R.P., JATMIKO, WAYHU SAPTOMO, E., and DUE, R.A., 2004. A new small-bodied hominin from the Late Pleistocene of Flores, Indonesia. Nature 431, 1055-1061.

CAMERON, D., PATNAIK, R. and SAHNI, A., 2004. The phylogenetic significance of the Middle Pleistocene Narmada Hominin Cranium from Central India. Internat. J. Osteoarchaeol. 14 (6), 419-447.

CARRETERO, J.M. ARSUAGA, J.L. and LORENZO, C., 1997. Clavicles, scapulae and humeri from the Simo de los Huesos site (Sierra de Atapuerca, Spain). J. Hum. Evol.33, 357-408.

CHATTERJEE, B.K., 1955. A comparative study of the different body proportions of the Onges of Little Andamans. The Anthropologist 2(2), 12-21.

CHESNER, C.A., ROSE, W.J., DRAKE, A.D.R. and WESTGATE, J.A., 1991. Eruptive history of earth's largest Quaternary Calderas (Toba, Indonesia) clarified. Geology 19, 200-203.

CHURCHILL, S.E., 1994. Human upper body evolution in the Eurasian Later Pleistocene. Ph.D. Dissertation, University of New Mexico.

deTERRA, P. and PATTERSON, T.T., 1939. Studies on the Ice Ages in India and associated human Cultures. Cong, Inst, Washington, Publ. 493, 313-326.

DUDAR, J.C., 1993. Identification of rib number and assessment of intercostals variation at the sternal rib end. J. Forens. Sci., JFSCA 38 (4), 788-797.

FLOWER, W.H., 1880. On the osteology and affinities of the natives of the Andaman Islands. J. Anthrop. Instt. (London) 9, 10-135.

FRANCISCUS, R.G. and CHURCHILL, S.E., 2002. The costal skeleton of Shanidar 3 and a reappraisal of Neandertal thoracic morphology. J. Hum. Evol. 42, 303-356.

GABUNIA, L., de LUMLEY, M-A., VEKUA, A., LORDKIPANIDZE, D. and de LUMLEY, H., 2002. Decouverte dun nouvel hominide a Dmanissi (Transcaucasie), Georgia). C. R. Palaevol. 1, 43-253.

JELLEMA, L.M., LATIMER, B. and WALKER, A., 1993. The Rib Cage. In: Walker, A. and Leakey, R. (eds), The Nariokotome Homo Erectus Skeleton. Cambridge, Harvard University Press, pp. 295-325.

JIT. I. and SINGH, S., 1956. Estimation of stature from clavicle. Ind. J. Med. Res. 44: 137-156.

JIT, I. and SINGH, S., 1966. The sexing of the adult clavicles. Ind. J. Med. Res. 54 (6), 551-571.

KENNEDY, K.A.R., 1992. The fossil hominin from the Narmada Valley: Homo erectus or Homo sapiens. In: Jarrige, C. (ed.), South Asian Archeology 1989, Prehistory Press, Madison, pp. 145-152.

KENNEDY, K.A.R., 1999. The Paleoanthropology of South Asia. Evol. Anthrop. 8, 157-194.

KENNEDY, K.A.R., 2000. God-Apes and Fossil men: The Paleoanthropology of South Asia. The University of Michigan Press, Michigan.

KENNEDY, K.A.R., SONAKIA, A., CHIMENT, J. and VERMA, K.K., 1991. Is the Narmada hominin an Indian Homo erectus? Am. J. Phys. Anthrop. 86, 475-496.

LUMLEY, H. de and SONAKIA, A., 1985. Contexte stratigraphique et Archaeologique de L'Homme de le Narmada, Hathnora, Madhya Pradesh, Inde. L'Anthropologie 89, 3-12.

LUMLEY, M.-A. de and SONAKIA, A., 1985. Premiere de coaverte d'un Homo erectus sur le continent Indien A. Hathnora, dans la Moyenne Vallee de la Narmada. L'Anthropologie 89, 13-61.

MISRA, S., VENKATESAN, T.R., RAJAGURU, S.N. and SOMAYAJULU, B.L.K., 1995. Earliest Acheulean Industry from peninsular India. Curr. Anthrop. 36 (5), 847-851.

PARSONS, F.G., 1916. On the proportions and characteristics of the modern English clavicle. J. Anat, 51, 71-93.

PEARSON, O.M., 2000. Activity, climate and postcranial robusticity: Implications for modern human origins and scenarios of adaptive change. Curr. Anthrop. 41 (4), 569-605.

RAO, K.V., CHAKRABARTI, S., RAO, K.J., RAMANI, M.S.V., MARATHE, S.D. and BORKAR, B.T., 1997. Magneto-stratigraphy of the Quaternary fluvial sediments and Tephra of Narmada Valley, Central India. In: Quaternary Geology of the Narmada Valley, Geol. Surv. India, Spl. Publn. No. 46, 65-78.

RIGHTMIRE, G.P., 1988. Homo erectus and later Middle Pleistocene humans. Ann. Rev. Anthropol. 117, 239-259.

SANKHYAN, A.R., 1985. Late occurrence of Sivapithecus in Indian Siwaliks. J. Hum. Evol. 14, 573-678.

SANKHYAN, A.R., 1997a. Fossil clavicle of a Middle Pleistocene hominin from the Central Narmada Valley, India. J. Hum. Evol. 32, 3-16.

SANKHYAN, A.R., 1997b. A new human fossil find from the Central Narmada basin and its chronology. Curr. Sci 73 (12), 1110-1111.

SANKHYAN, A.R., 1999. The place of Narmada hominin in the Jigsaw puzzle of human origins. In: M.P. Tiwari and D.M. Mohabey (eds.), Quaternary of India, Gondvana Geol. Magz. Spl. Publ. 4, pp. 335-345.

SANKHYAN, A.R. 2005. New fossils of early Stone Age Man from central Narmada Valley. Current Science 88 (5). 704-707.

SHAUFFER, I.A. and COLLINS, W.V., 1966. The deep clavicular rhomboid fossa. J. Am. Med. Assoc. 195, 158-159.

SONAKIA, A., 1984. The skull cap of Early Man and associated mammalian fauna from Narmada Valley Alluvium, Hoshangabad area, M.P. (India). Rec. Geol. Surv, India, 113, 159-172.

TIWARI, M.P., 2005. Correlation of Lithostratigraphy and Chronology of the Narmada Valley Quaternary. In: A.R. Sankhyan and V.R. Rao (eds), Human Origins in India: Contemporary Perspectives. Anthropological Survey of India, Calcutta (In Press).

TIWARI, M.P. and BHAI H.Y., 1997. Quaternary stratigraphy of the Narmada Valley. In: Quaternary Geology of the Narmada Valley, Geol. Surv. Ind. Spl. Pulb. No. 46, 33-63.

TRINKAUS, E., 1983. The Shanidar Neandertals. Academic Press, New York.

VANDERMEERSCH, B., 1981. Les hommes Fessiles de Qafzeh (Isarael), C.N.R.S., Paris.

VANDERMEERSCH, B., 1991. La Ceinture scapulaire et les members Superieurs., In: Yosef, O.B. and Vandermeersch, B. (eds), Le Squelette Mousterien de Kebara 2. CNRS, Paris, pp.157-159.

VANDERMEERSCH, B. and TRINKAUS, E., 1995. The postcranial remains of the Regourdou 1 Neandertal: The shoulder and arm remains. J. Hum. Evol. 28, 439 – 476.

VRBA, E.S., 1979. A new study of the scapula of *Australopithecus africanus* from Sterkfontein. Am. J. Phys. Anthrop. 16, 351-377.

WALKER, A.C. and LEAKEY, R.E.F. (eds), 1993. The Nariokotome *Homo erectus* skeleton. Harvard University Press, Boston.

UNDERSTANDING ACHEULIAN CULTURE IN THE GANDHESWARI RIVER VALLEY, BANKURA, WEST-BENGAL, INDIA

Asok DATTA

Department of Archaeology, Calcutta University, 1, Reformatory Street, Kolkata 700 027, India.
E-mail: akd19@rediffmail.com

Abstract: The Indian lower Palaeolithic is characterized by two cultural or technical traditions viz. the Soanian of the north-west and the Acheulian of the peninsular India. The Soanian is characterized by Pebble tools (Chopper/Chopping) and other types while the Acheulian is identified on the basis of Handaxes and other tool types. They are considered separate, but at times temporally overlapping artifact types are found. The Acheulian culture in India, in its eastern migration, did not cross the vast alluvium corridor of Bengal basin which comprises 63% of the total land mass of West-Bengal and more than 90% of the total land mass of Bangladesh . Naturally the geological history of undivided Bengal is the history of filling this basinal area with sediments brought from Ganga and Brahmaputra rivers. The process started from Neogene period and it is still an ongoing process. Only the Chotonagpur Plateau fringe area in West-Bengal covering the districts of Purulia, western part of Bankura and South-Western part of West-Midnapur are enormously rich in Palaeolithic and later Stone Age materials.
Gandheswari, a tributary of Dwarakeswar, is a small river (32 K.M) flowing in the north-south direction in Bankura district near the foothills of Susunia, an isolated and weathered remnant of former continuous plateau chain. Gandheswari near Susunia hill was the breeding ground of Acheulian culture in Bankura district. More than forty five Acheulian sites with thousands of artifacts have been reported from this river valley. The industry comprises Handaxe, Cleaver, Chopper, Scraper, Flake, Core; etc. Besides the region has also yielded a large quantity of animal fossil vertebrates from Pleistocene sediments and in many cases along with Acheulian artifacts. The fossil remains mostly belonged to mammal and reptile groups. The present paper attempts to reconstruct the Acheulian settlement system of Gandheswari river valley during the Pleistocene time period on the basis of clustering of Acheulian sites, artifacts and animal fossil vertebrates.
Keywords: Acheulian, Soanian, Gangheswari river, Susunia hill, Handaxe, Cleaver, Chopper, Chopping Chotonagpur Plateau, Secondary Laterite, Fossil vertebrates, Primary, Secondary and Tertiary sites, Core area, dispersed area, hot and dry open land

Résumé: Le Paléolithique inférieur Indien est caractérisé par deux traditions culturelles ou deux traditions techniques, le Soanien du nor-ouest et l'Acheuléen de l'Inde péninsulaire. Le Soanien est caractérisé par des galets aménagés (Chopper/Chopping) et d'autre types, alors que l'Acheuléen est identifié sur la bse des bifaces et d'autres outils. Ils sont considérés séparément, mais parfois des types d'artéfacts sont trouvés temporallement superimposés. La culture Acheuléenne en Inde, dasn sa migration vers l'Est, n'a pas croisé le corridor du vaste alluvium du basin du Bengal, lequel comprends le 63% de toute la masse de terre du Bengal Occidental et plus de 90% de toute la masse de terre du Bangladesh. Naturellement, l'histoire géologique du Bengal indivisé c'est l'histoire du remplissage de ce bassin avec des sédiments des fleuves Ganga et Brahmaputra. Le processus a démarré au Néogène et se poursuit toujours. Seul l'estrême du plateau de Chotonagpur, dans le Bengal occidental, couvrant les départements de Purulia, la partie occidentale de Bankura et la partir Sudouest du Midnapur Occidental, est extremement riche en matériaux du Paléolithique et l'Âge d ela Pierre final.
Le Gandheswari, un affluent du Dwarakeswar, est un petit fleuve (32 Km) qui coule Nord-Sud dans la direction du département de Bankura, auprès du piémont de Susunia, un reste isolé et érodé d'une ancienne chaine applatie. Gandheswari auprès de Susunia fut le territoire pour la culture Acheuléenne dans le département de Bankura. Plus de quarante cinq sites avec des milliers de artéfactes furent reportés dans cette vallée. L'industrie comprens des bifaces, des hachereaux, des racloirs, des éclats, des nucléus, etc. Aussi, la région a livré une grande quantité de fossiles d'animaux vertébrés, dans les sédiments du Pleistocène et, en plusieurs cas, associés à des artefactes Acheuléens. Les restes fossiles appartiennent surtout a des mamifères et des reptiles. Cet article éssaye de reconstruire le système d'habitat achéuléen de la vallée du Gandheswari pendant le Pleistocène, sur la base de cluster de sites acheuléens, des artefactes et des fossiles de vertébrés.
Mots-clés: Acheuléen, Soanien, fleuve Gangheswari, mont Susunia, Biface, Hachereau, Chopper, Chopping, plateau de Chotonagpur, laterite secondaire, vertebrés fossiles, sites primaires, secondaire et tertiaires, aire noyau, aire dispersée, paysage ouvert chaud et sec

INTRODUCTION

The lower Palaeolithic culture in India is characterized by two cultural or technical traditions viz. the Soanian and the Acheulian (Misra, 2001).The Soanian or the soan culture was confined to north India and Pakistan while the Acheulian is found to be distributed over a wide region. The Acheulian cultural remains have been reported from the siwalik in the north to Chennai in the south (Paddayya, 1984; Misra, 1989; Sen, 1955) and Gujrat in the west to West-Bengal in the east (Ghosh, 1966; Datta, 1979; 1982) except the alluvium corridor within this broad canvas of the region (Ghosh and Chakraborty, 1975). The Soanian is characterized by pebble tools (Chopper/Chopping) and scrapers, flakes, blades and cores (Misra, 2001; Sankalia, 1974). The Acheulian on the other hand is identified on the basis of Handaxes, the shape of which varies from pear, ovate, triangular, cordate, lanceolate and transitional forms between them and pebble tools, Scraper, cleaver flakes, blades and cores. These are considered separate, but at times temporally overlapping artifact types are found (Misra, 2001). The Handaxes are often described as "all purpose tool". But its actual functions are often fraught with contradictions. The earliest known Handaxe from definite stratigraphical context at bed II, Olduvai Gorge in east Africa has been dated to 1.3 million years old (Wymer, 1982). However its vertical sequence anywhere in the old world does not confirm any evolutionary change over time. The best symmetrical forms are found together with the crudely chipped handaxes both in Africa and India (Wymer, 1982; Pappu, 2004) suggesting thereby no evolutionary sequence of the types in its vertical spread. The Acheulian is traditionally associated with cylinder hammer technique. But the initial preparation of the tool was made by stone hammer while soft hammer or cylinder hammer technique was applied for achieving the bilateral symmetry of the tool.

The Soanian in India is dated to 300.000 years old (Mahapatra, 1976) while the Acheulian is dated to 0,67+0.03 million years old at Bori (Misra, 2001), but a more secure date of the Acheulian has been obtained at Didwana in Rajasthan (Misra and Rajguru, 1986) and Umrethi in Gujrat (Marathe, 1981), which suggest the Acheulian as 200.000 years old. The Acheulian in India is associated with fossil vertebrates of Bos namadicus, Elephas namadicus, Sus namadicus, Elephas hysudricus, Hexaprodon namadicus, Stegodon insignis etc, which are believed to be of middle Pleistocene age (De Terra and Paterson, 1939; Badam, 1984). The fossil materials together with the artifacts reveal the kind of Palaeo-landscape in which the Acheulian people of India lived and survived through interactions.

GEOGRAPHICAL SETTINGS OF THE STUDY AREA

The present study area is the Gandheswari river valley in Bankura district. Bankura is one of the few districts in West-Bengal, which has yielded rich prehistoric cultural materials. The prehistoric culture of Gandheswari river valley is characterized by Acheulian culture that is dominated by Handaxe industry. The total area of the district is 2,647square mile that accounts to7.91% of the total landmass of West-Bengal. The density population of the district is 627 per square mile against 1032 in the state. The forest coverage of the district is 20.04% while the major flora and fauna of the district comprise *Sal, Asan, Bahara, Piasal, Palas, Kend etc and Leopard, Jungle cat, Jackal, Fox, Bear* and different types of birds and reptiles. Geomorphologically the district can broadly be divided into three units viz. the hilly country of the west, the undulating red soil area of the center and the alluvium flat land in the east. The hilly area of the west in the district is basically an extension of Chotonagpur plateau fringe area. Isolated hills in this region are relics of erosion and denudation of the former plateau. Biharinath with 447.08 M and Susunia with 439.05 M heights stand isolated in the region. There are other smaller hills of moderate heights in the region. These residual flat-topped low hills of Precambrian age are deeply weathered forming lateritic crust at the top. These isolated denudational hills are often surrounded by an erosional plain surface developed over the denuded Precambrian rocks and Jurassic volcano (Rajmohal trap). This peneplain has occasional rock exposures and is partly covered by insitu primary laterite and partly insitu residual soil developed over the basement rocks. The plain is moderately dissected and has an easterly slope and occupies a level of 80-260 M from the MSL. There are older rocks of the Achaean system like Dolerite, Pegmatite, Granite, Gneiss, Schist Quartzite, and Limestone etc. while the Gondwana system includes Sandstone and Shale stone. The Pleistocene activities are recorded in the form of laterite and gravel formations while the recent deposits are alluvium soil. The major rivers of the district are Damodar, Dwarakeswar, Sali and Gandheswari etc. Gandheswari is a tributary of Dwarakeswar, which originates in the north/western part of Chatna police station and while covering its 32 km length from source to mouth it passes through Chatna and Bankura before merges with Dwarakeswar in Bankura. The district is rich in ethnographic data, which comprises Ho, Lodha, Munda and Oran etc., but they are found in variable number (Cencus, 1961).

STRATIGRAPHY

There is not a single river section, which contains the sequential ordering of the Pleistocene, and post-pleistocene sedimentations in the southwestern part of West-Bengal where the palaeolithic or stone age cultures are generally found to be present. Hence, the river stratigraphy as worked out by different scholars in different times is a composite one and based on observations of different sections at different places (Ghosh, 1998).

A thick deposit of mottled clay is found sometime directly resting on bedrock generally in areas where the existing minerals and rocks are very soft and in some other areas, particularly in the hard rock area, the mottled clay bed is totally absent. This mottled clay bed is succeeded by a highly lateritized boulder conglomerate bed having both bigger and smaller gravels. A silty clay bed succeeds this bed and at the top of this clay bed there is another gravel bed, which is loose and unconsolidated and smaller in size (Ghosh, 1998). The angularity of these gravels does not suggest long distance transportation while the roundness of forms of the earlier gravel bed suggests long distance transportation. The second gravel bed is again succeeded by a silt bed and at the top of which lies the recent alluvium deposits. This kind of situation can be observed in the main rivers, but during the same period of time, the tributary rivers of the south-western part of west-Bengal shows altogether a different river stratigraphy. It shows that immediately above the bedrock there is huge deposit of secondary laterite, which is often implementiferrous. This detrital laterite contains pisolithic nodules, gravels and other rock fragments. This bed is succeeded by a silty bed and at the top of which lies the recent alluvium deposits. The Palaeolithic or the Acheulian artifacts in West-Bengal are found either in the gravel bed of the main river or in the detrital laterite bed of the tributaries of the main rivers. But no attempt has been made by any scholar to correlate between the deposits. In fact, we do not have any minimum idea about the dating of these clustic sediments. However since these sediments also yielded a large number of fossil vertebrates that roughly belonged to upper pleistocene, we can assume an idea about the date of the tools found from these deposits. The approximate date is between 100.000 to 50.000 years old. The above stratigraphical sequence relates to the amount of precipitation that causes wet and dry phases and also temperature and humidity (Ghosh, 1998). It can be assumed that bigger clustic sediments indicate higher precipitation and thereby increasing the volume and velocity of water in rivers whereas smaller sediments indicate less precipitation and thereby causing decrease the volume and velocity of river water. We can conclude therefore that the major rivers due to substantial increase of water are often subjected to flood and thereby destroying the archaeological materials. But in sharp contrast the tributary rivers due to less water are not often subjected to seasonal flood and thereby preserving the archaeological materials in its original position. So, tributary rivers offer very potential scope to reconstruct the cultural life of the people who lived along its bank. Gandheswari is a tributary of Dwarakeswar. The Acheulian way of life can be reconstructed, to a great extent, on the basis of cultural materials as well the faunal remains found from the this region.

PREVIOUS WORK

The first palaeolithic tool in eastern India was collected by Valentine Ball in 1865 and again in 1867 from the Bankura district in West-Bengal and since then it became a center of attraction of palaeolithic research. V.D. Krishnaswami undertook the first systematic survey relating to palaeolithic study during the year 1959-1960 in the middle course of Kasai river which passes through the southern part of Bankura and Purulia districts and discovered a number of palaeolithic sites mainly from Kumari and Jam rivers, both are tributaries of Kasai. In 1962 D. Sen explored the middle course of Dwarakeswar river near Bankura town and reported few palaeolithic sites along with artifacts that comprise pebble chopper/ chopping and handaxe, cleaver, scraper, flake etc. However, the Gandheswari river, which is the prime focus in the present context, was first explored by P.C. Dasgupta in 1964. Dasgupta through his painstaking work discovered no less than forty palaeolithic sites and the artifacts collected from those sites amount to few thousand. Dasgupta (Dasgupta, 1967) did not pay much attention to the geo-stratigraphy of the region. However, on the other hand it was mainly due to his persistent research efforts either through writings or publicity that Susunia came to the lime light of prehistoric research in India. Susunia offers a unique field for prehistoric

research. But the most interesting feature of the prehistoric culture of the area is the complete dominance of handaxe industry, which is never ever reported from any place any where in India. It needs a fresh investigation in view of the predominant character of Handaxe in the industry. Besides, a number of other Scholars have also worked in this area (Chattopadhyay, 1992; Datta, 2002; Chakraborty, 1993 etc.).

DISTRIBUTION OF SITES AND INDUSTRIAL ASSEMBLAGES

The landscape of Gandheswari river valley is dominated by the magnificent and majestic hump shaped Susunia hill (23 22 30 north latitude and 86 58 20 east longitude) which occupies an area of 24 square km. The Acheulian life revolved round this hill. More than 55 Acheulian sites have been identified so far in this region (Fig. 3.1) The artifact assemblage comprises chopper/chopping tools, handaxe, cleaver scraper, sling ball, flake and core etc. These Acheulian artifacts are believed to have served a variety of functions like hunting, butchering, skinning of animals, shattering and breaking of bones for marrow, digging of roots, tubers, processing of plant foods and making of wooden tools and weapons (Misra, 2001). In the making of these artifacts both stone hammer and cylinder hammer techniques were applied. Cylinder hammer technique was extensively used to obtain bilateral symmetry of the handaxes. The Levalloisian technique is however found to be absent in this region. But the most conspicuous feature of the industry is the complete dominance of handaxes, which is always more than 90% in every site. Total number of artifacts collected from this region is 1775, of which handaxes comprise 1686 representing 94.98% in the total collection. The other artifacts like chopper, cleaver, scraper; sling ball, flake and core together comprise 5.01 %. This shows the dominant character of the handaxe in the industry.

Among the other types, both chopper and cleaver together comprise only 0.78% while scraper has a slight higher percentage of 1.40. The situation seems to be very conspicuous in the sense that the by product or debitage or waste material of an industry of such dimension should have, at least, higher percentage of waste materials which is totally absent in the present case. The only explanation in the present case is that the previous explorers did not pay much attention to collect waste materials.

All the data used in the present paper have been complied from A.C. Pal's Prehistory of Susunia hill complex and the Suvarnarekha valley, 1996, Directorate of Archaeology, West Bengal; D. Ray's Bone implements from Bhaluksoda cave, Susunia, 1991 in Studies in Archaeology, Ed. A. Datta, New Delhi, pp.59-65; B.D. Chattopadhya and other's: An annotated Archaeological Atlas of West Bengal. Vol.1, Prehistory and Protohistory, Directorate of Archaeology, West Bengal. 2005, Kolkata: P.C. Dasgupta;s Pragaitihasik Susunia, Directorate of Archaeo-

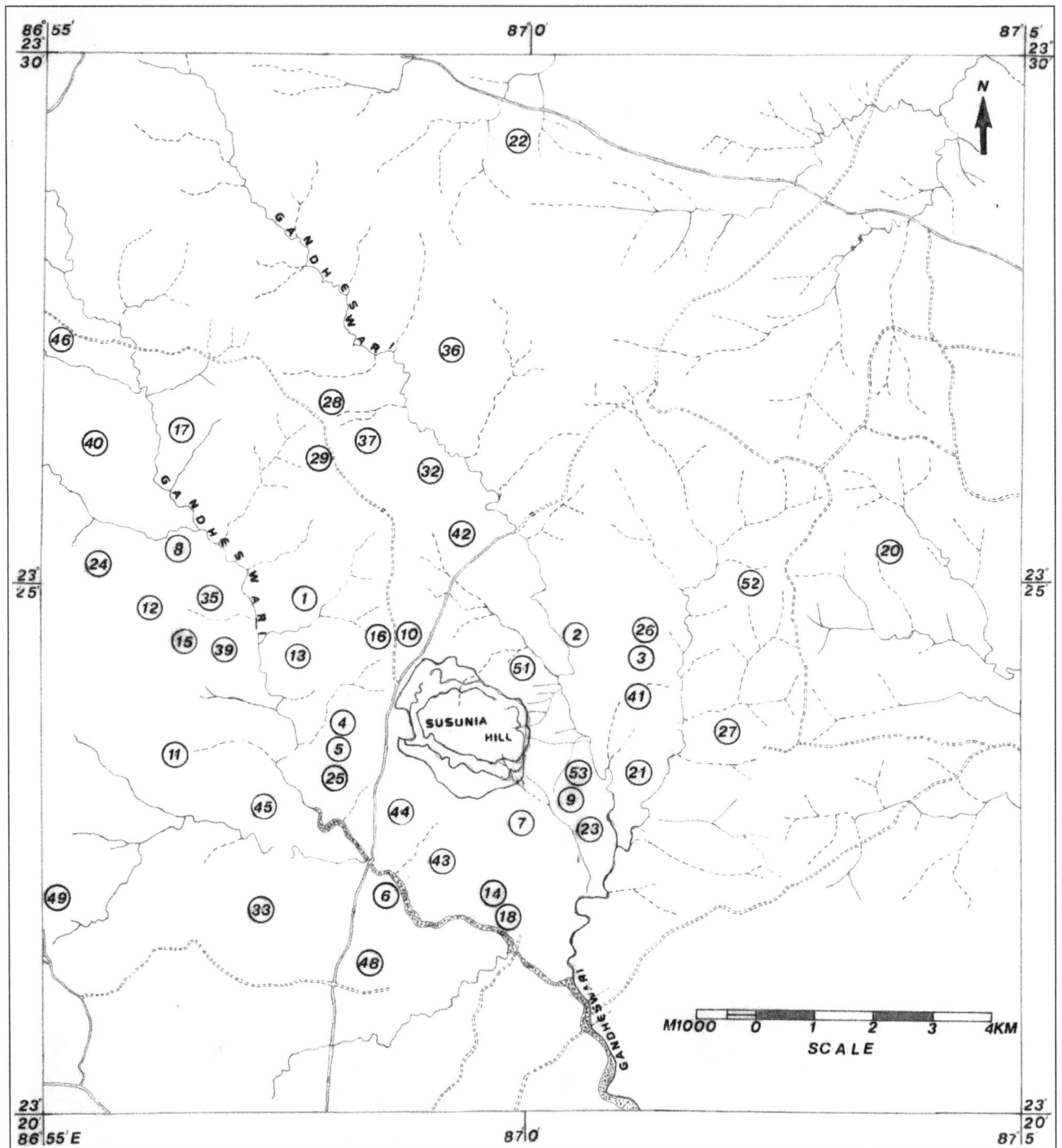

Fig. 3.1. Distribution of Acheulian sites in Gandheswari River valley

logy, West-Bengal, 1967; Indian Archaeology-A review. 1960-1981.

Handaxes are made on both on pebble, core and flake, but handaxes made on core are having a higher percentage. Handaxes are always provided with additional flake scares that are small and shallow forming bilateral symmetry. There are extensive secondary retouching on the sides of the artifact to make them perfectly symmetrical. Handaxes on fkake are also not common, and does not form a very substantial percentage while

Handaxes on pebble are few. Among the shapes almond, pear, ovate, triangular and lanceolate are very common in the industry. In case of raw material, quartzite is the dominant type, which forms 98.06 percent while quartz and sandstone are also present but their respective percentages are 1.08 and 0.84. Quartzite is available in the form of river pebble as well outcrops, which are visible at a number of places in the river valley. The gravel bed, which yielded Acheulian artifacts, also contains rich animal fossil vertebrates that include *Trionxy gangeticus*, *Hystrix crassidons*, *Bos indicus*, *Bos namadicus*, *Bos*

	SPECIES	Total Sites	NO	%	
Antilope Cervicapra (Black Buck)					
Muntiacus Muntjak (Barking deer)	Deer	15	10	22.72	
Axis axis (Swamp deer)					
Cervus unicolor (Sambar)					
Trioxy gangeticus	Turtle	15	4	9.09	
Boselaphus namadicus / Boselaphus sp.	Nilgai	15	4	9.09	
Bos indicus / Bos namadicus / Bos namadicus bengalensis	Cattle	15	8	18.18	
Elephas namadicus / Elephas maximus	Elephant	15	2	4.54	
Gavialus gangeticus	Gharial	15	3	6.81	
Hystrix crassidons	porcupine	15	3	6.81	
Equus anager khur	Wild Ass	15	2	4.54	
Bubalus bubalus palaeo indicus	Buffalo	15	1	2.27	
Giraffa cf. cameloportalis	Giraffe	15	1	2.27	
Sus scrofa cristatus	Pig	15	1	2.27	
Canis familiarus	Dog	15	1	2.27	
Panthera cf. leo	Lion	15	2	4.54	
Panthera cf. leo pordus	Leopard	15	1	2.27	
Cracuta sp.	Hyena	15	1	2.27	

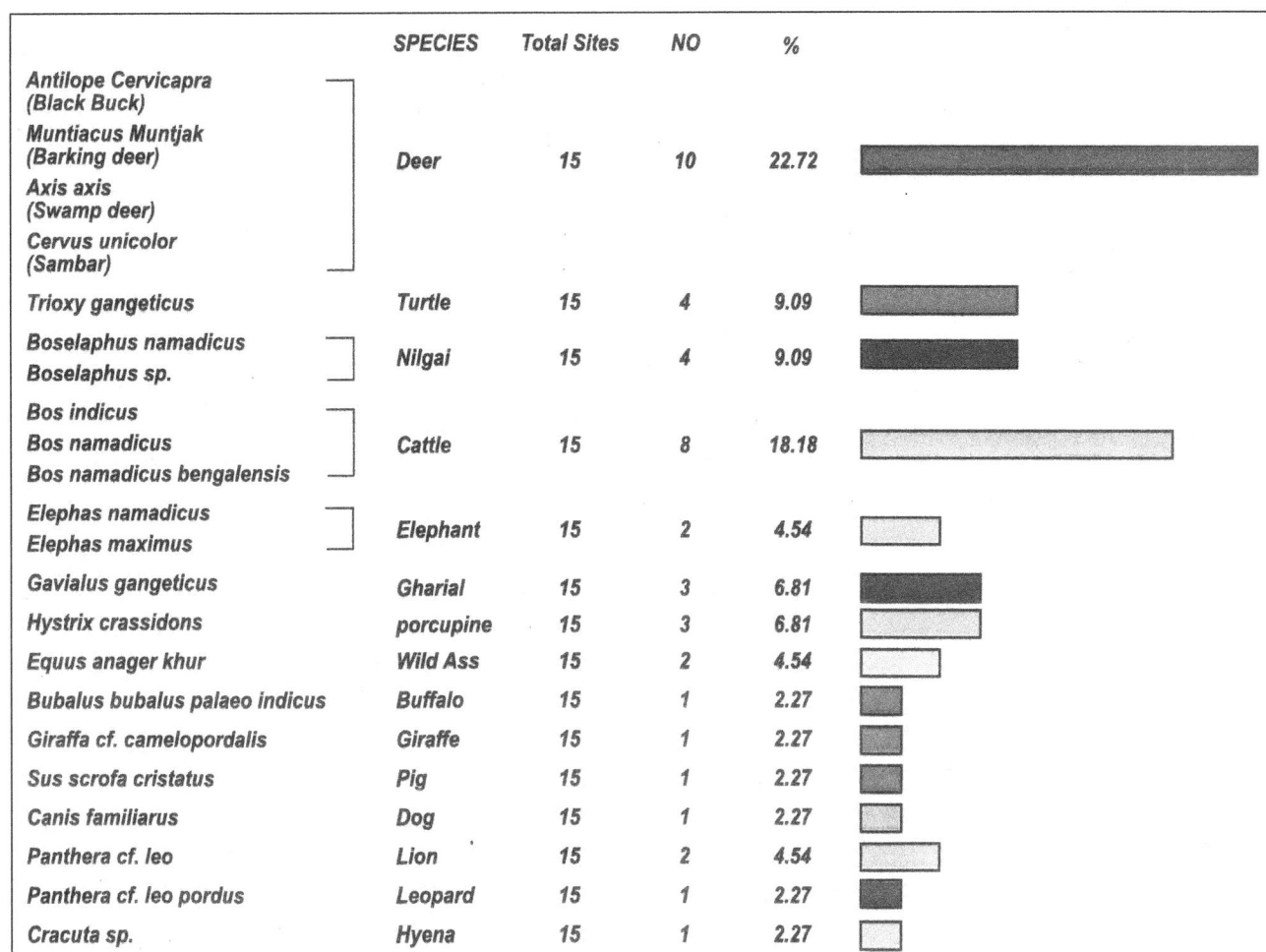

Fig. 3.2. Distribution of animal remains, Gandheswari River valley

namadicus bengalensis, Boselaphus namadicus, Boslephus sp., Bubalus bubalus palaeoindicus, Antilope cervicapra, Muntiacus muntjak, Axix axix, Cervus duvauceli, Cervus Unicolor, Giraffa cf. cameloportalis, Panthera cf. leo, Panthera cf leo pordus, crocuta sp, Canis familiarus, Elephus namadicus, Gavialus gageticus, Equus anager khur, Palaeoloxodon sp., Elephus maximus etc. (Davis, 1987; Datta, 2002, Datta, 1976, Banerjee and Ghosh, 1977, Ghosh, Saha, Saha Ray and Talukder, 1992) *These fossil materials include both reptile and mammal groups which possibly formed the food items or one of the major source of subsistence economy. The fossil materials represent the upper Pleistocene period. This is assumed on the basis of the fact that the fossil materials contains both extinct and present forms, and it is likely that the present form did not evolve after 35.000 years age. So, we can tentatively date the Acheulian of the Gandheswari river valley between 100.000 to 50.000 years old.*

SETTLEMENT SYSTEM

On the basis of frequency of artifacts, the Acheulian sites in the Gandheswari river valley can be classified into three categories viz. primary sites, secondary sites and tertiary sites. The sites, which yielded 100 and above artifacts are called here as primary sites. There are six sites of this category. The sites that yielded artifacts between 20 to 100 are called secondary sites. There are 10 sites of this category. The sites that yielded artifacts between 1 to 20 are called tertiary sites. There are 39 sites of this category (Fig. 3.2). The total collection of artifacts from all these categories of sites is 1775, in which handaxe comprises 94.98 percent indicating a very exceptional area of Acheulian culture. The six primary sites identified on the basis of the above bench mark has yielded 1146 artifacts representing 61.40 percent in the total collection and 64.65 percent in the collection of handaxes. Similarly, the ten secondary sites yielded a total of 402 artifacts representing 22.64 percent in the total collection and 22.53 in the collection of handaxes. In the same time 39 tertiary sites yielded a total of 227 artifacts representing 12.78 percent in the total collection and 12.81 in the collection of Handaxes.

The Acheulian life in the Gandheswar river valley revolved rounds the Susunia hill. Because the Acheulian sites are found all around the susunia hill. On the basis of clustering of sites, density distribution of artifacts,

29

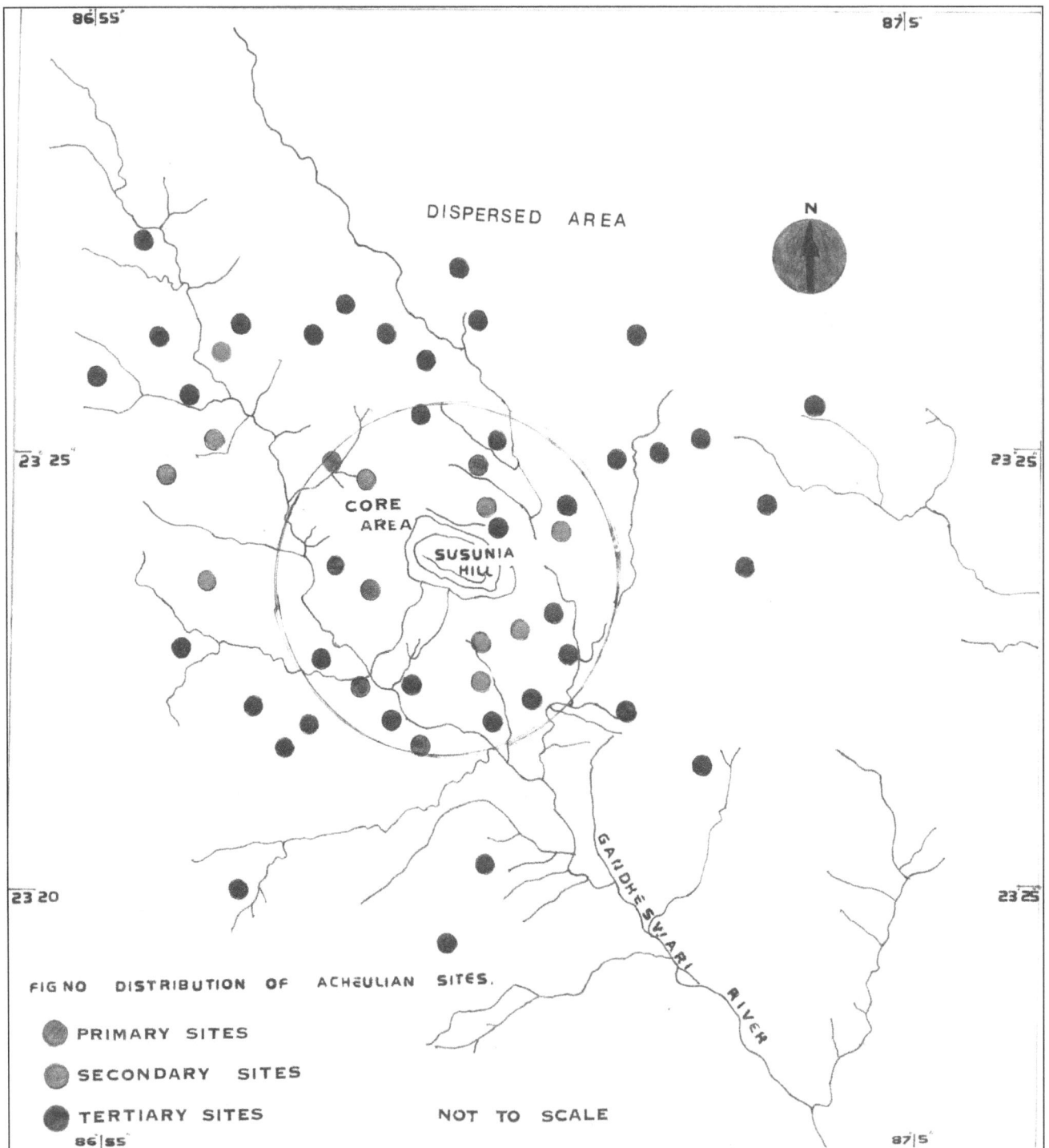

Fig. 3.3. Distribution of primary, secondary and tertiary sites

location and distance from the hill, two different types of settlement areas have been identified viz. the core area and the dispersed area. All the primary sites are located within an area of 3.5 k.m radius from the center of the susunia hill. Besides, six secondary and eleven tertiary sites are located within this area. Hence we call the area as core area. The total number of sites found in the core area is 23, which yielded altogether 1530 artifacts, which means that the percentage of tools in the core area is 86.19. But in sharp contrast, the total number of sites outside this core area is 32, which yielded only 245 artifacts representing only 13.80 percent in the total collection. We, can therefore suggest that the core area having 5 km radius from the susunia hill is the basic settlement area of the Acheulian people of the Gandheswari river valley while the vast area lying outside this core area and which has yielded 32 sites with 245 artifacts representing only 13.80 percent of the total collection may be termed as dispersed area used for hunting and temporary shelter of the people during wet season.

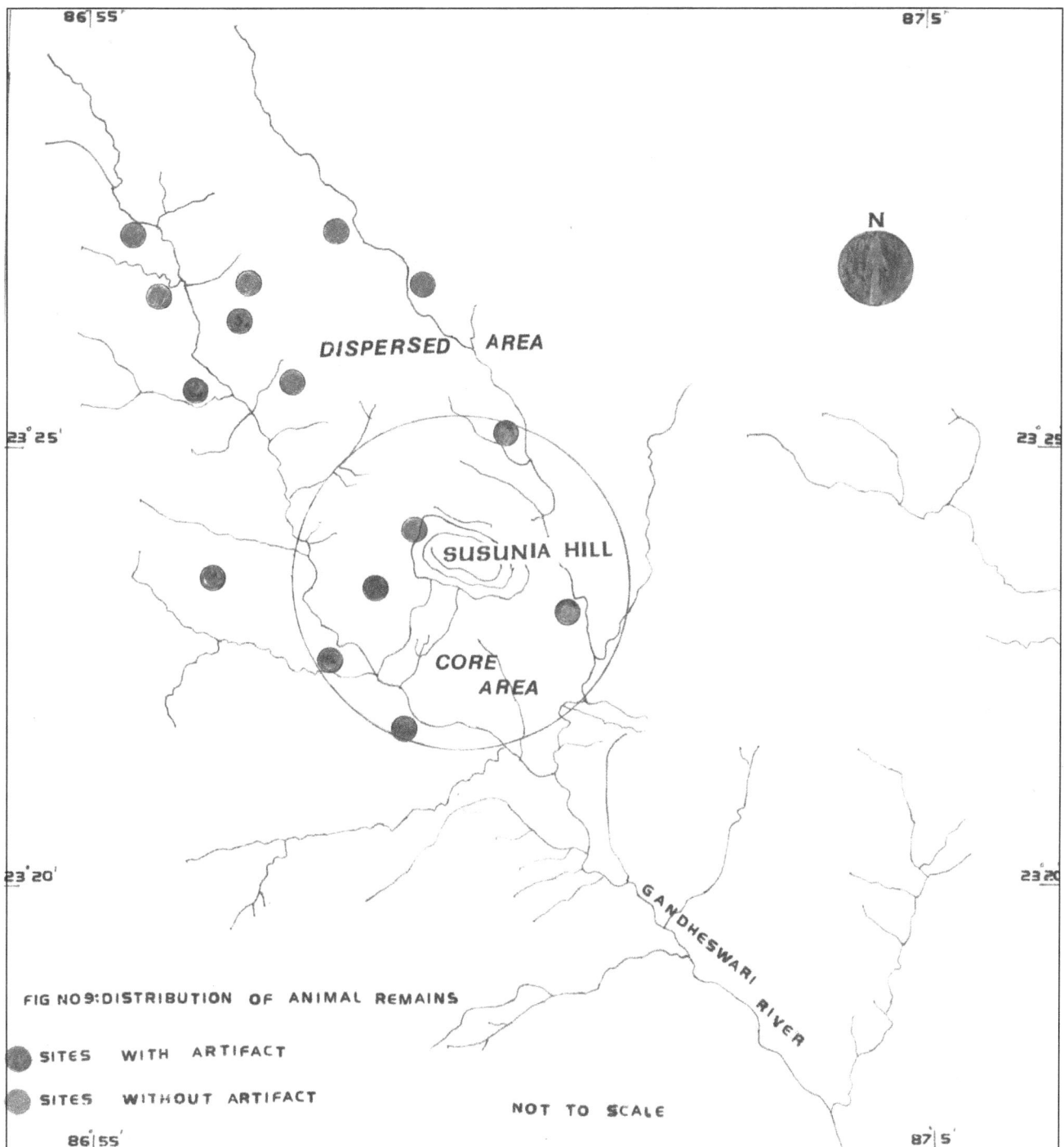

Fig. 3.4. Distribution of fossil bearing sites

Animal fossil vertebrates have been reported from fifteen sites in the Gandheswari river valley (Fig. 3.3), of which ten fossil bearing sites are directly associated with Acheulian tools. Again in the core area, there are six fossil bearing sites and of these three sites are found associated with Acheulian artifacts. In the dispersed area there area nine fossil bearing sites, of which four are associated with Acheulian artifacts while the remaining five are without any archaeological context, but strongly suggest its close association with the contemporary Acheulian culture, because the species are similar and identical.

Among the species identified, the ratio of carnivores to herbivores is 1:3. This ratio reflects the type of ecosystem that existed in the Gandheswari river valley during the Acheulian time. The analysis shows that animal species comprising Giraffe, lion, leopard, hyena, nilgai, deer, cattle etc. contributing almost 64.47 percent, prefer hot, dry highland with scrub, bushes, grasses and isolated trees while animal species comprising buffalo, elephant, gharial, turtle, pig etc contributing 25 percent, prefer warm, humid reverie landscape with swampy grassland and moderate forest coverage (Datta, 2000). Similarly porcupine and wild ass prefer hot, dry semi-arid land (Fig. 3.4).

It appears therefore that the general landscape of Gandheswari river valley during Acheulian time was characterized by hot and dry open land with grass, bushes and isolated trees. The settlement system of the Acheulian people can be classified into two types viz. the dry season settlement and the wet season settlement (Fig. 3.2). In the dry season, the Acheulian people concentrated in the core area. Because during the month of summer, the adjoining areas of susunia hill, the area become extremely dry due to high temperature and humidity. The rivers, nullas, streams and all other water sources and water holes in the region become dry and empty. The situation did not change much even today. There are no natural springs, no water sources to sustain life in this rugged, hot and dry area in those days. It is even very difficult, in these days despite modern means of mechanism, to sustain life. Naturally there were migrations of both men and animals more towards the susunia hill during this time. On the other hand, what we call here as the core area, is protected by moderate forest coverage with plenty of plant food, animal resources and perineal water supply, raw materials, caves and rock shelters and such other things which are required for survival. This might have attracted the Acheulian people to settle there not only in the dry period but also during the wet phase. It was only during this wet phase that the Acheulian people extended their subsistence base beyond their core settlement area. We can therefore conclude that the Acheulian culture at Gandheswari river valley was characterized by two types of settlement system viz. the wet season and the dry season settlements which were needed for survival mechanism.

References

BADAM, G.L., 1984: Pleistocene faunal succession in India. In: The evolution Of east Asian Environment. Ed. R.O. White. PP.746-775.

BALL, VALENTINE, 1865: Stone implements found in Bengal. Proceeding of Asiatic Society of Bengal. PP.127-128. Kolkata.

BALL, VALENTINE, 1867: Note on stone implements in Bengal. Proceeding of Asiatic Society of Bengal. Kolkata. PP.143.

BANERJEE, S. and M. GHOSH, 1977: On the occurrence of Giraffe cf. cameloopordalis from the Prehistoric site of Susunia, Bankura, West-Bengal. Science and culture. Vol. 43:368-370. Kolkata.

DASGUPTA, P.C., 1964: Pragoitihasik Susunia. West-Bengal Govt. Publication Kolkata.

CHATTOPADHYAY, R.K., 1992: Palaeolithic West-Bengal. Pratnasamiksha. Vol.1:27-60 Kolkata.

DATTA, A., 1976: Occurrence of fossil lion and spotted hyena in Pleistocene Deposits of Susunia, Bankura,

West-Bengal. Journal of the Geological Society. Vol. 17(13): 386-391. Kolkata.

DATTA, A., 1982: Palaeohistory of Man and his Culture. AgamKala Prakashan. Delhi.

DATTA, A., 1979: Pebble-Core element in India- A study on Geo-Cultural Variation. Ph.D Thesis. Calcutta University.

DATTA, A., 2002: Ecology and Cultural behavior of early men in Bengal: A Case study at Gandheswari and Tarafeni river valleys. In: Archaeology of Eastern India: New perspectives. Eds. Sengupta and Panja. Caste. Kolkata.

DAVIS, J.N. SIMON, 1987: The Archaeology of Animals. Batsford. London.

DE TERRA and T.T. PATERSON, 1939: Studies in Ice age in India and associated human cultures Washington D.C Carnegie Institute of Washington Publication No 499.

GHOSH, A.K., and CHAKRABORTY, D.K., 1975: Prehistoric research in India: Perspective in Cultural History. Varia. Vol. 24(1-2) 159-175. Hungary.

GHOSH, A.K, 1966: Palaeolithic cultures in West-Bengal. Bulletin of the Cultural Research Institute. 5(1-3) 83-93. Kolkata.

GHOSH, A.K., and others, 1998: Palaeolithic Industries of Eastern India: A new venture for comprehension. In: History and Archaeology of Eastern India. Ed. Asok Datta. PP.79-96. Kolkata.

GHOSH, M, SAHA, K.D., and others, 1981: Archaeo-zoological remains from West-Bengal. State Fauna Series: Fauna of West Bengal. Zoological Survey of India. Vol. 2:349-381.

MAHAPATRA, G.C., 1976: Geotectonic development, sub-Himalayan lithic complex and post Siwalik sediments. In: Perspective in Palaeo-Anthropology. Ed. Ghosh. PP.31-59. Kolkata.

MARATHE, A.R., 1981: Geoarchaeology of Hiran Valley, Sourastha, India. Deccan College. Pune.

MISRA, V.N and S.N. RAJGURU, 1986: Environment et culture del'Homme Prehistorique dans Le desert du Thar, Rajasthan. Inde.L'Antropologie. 90(3): 407-437.

MISRA, V.N., 1989: Stone age India: An Ecological perspective. Man and Environment. 14:17-64. Pune.

MISRA, V.N., 2001: Archaeological evidence of early modern human occupation In South Asia. In: Humanity fromAfrican Naissance to Coming Millennia. Eds. Phillip Tobias, Raath, MaggiCecchi and Doyle. South Africa. PP. 223-229.

PADDAYYA, K., 1984: Old stone age in India.In: New forschuengen zur alysteineit. Ed. H.Mullar Karpe. PP.445-493. Munchen.

PAPPU, S., and others, 2004: Preliminary report on excavation at the prehistoric site of Attirampakkam, Tamil Nadu (1999-2004. Man and Environment. Vol. XXIX (2): 1-17. Pune.

SANKALIA, S.D., 1974: Prehistory and Protohistory of India and Pakistan. Pune. Deccan College.

SEN, D., 1955: Nalagarh Palaeolithic Culture. Man in India. 35(3):177-184. Ranchi.

WYMER, J., 1982: Palaeolithic age. Croom Helm LTD. London.

PREHISTORIC RESEARCH IN BENGAL –
ON THE THRESHOLD

Bishnupriya BASAK

Department of Archaeology, Calcutta University, Kolkata, India

Abstract: The western upland (comprising Purulia, and the western parts of Birbhum, Bankura, Burdwan and Midnapur) in the state of West Bengal is a potential region for prehistoric research. Earlier studies in the region have been a valuable source of information, although throwing up major lacuna. An attempt is made here to explain the changing status of prehistoric research in Bengal with the help of two case studies. In the first - undertaken as a part of Ph. D dissertation - microlithic sites were studied within a regional approach. A holistic understanding of human behaviour was sought through a study of the distribution of sites and through an intensive analysis of the reduction procedure. Ethnography was used as an insight to understand past strategies of land use. A multidisciplinary approach was adopted for the study of the context that yielded preliminary information on the palaeoenvironment. In the second - part of an ongoing research - one is trying to see how far past perceptions of landscape can be seen from the locations of microlithic sites and a study of their assemblage, situating this in the backdrop of recent studies in which landscape emerges as a culturally constructed phenomenon. Ethnography is used as a tool for different ends—to assess how far it can offer insights into past perceptions.
Keywords: microlithic, processual, reduction procedure, landscape, post-processual, ethnography, perception

Résumé: Les terres hautes occidentals (y compris Purulia et les parties occidentales de Birbhum, Nakura, Burdwan et Midnapur) dans l'État de Bengal occidental, est une région potentielle pour la recherche préhistorique. Des études préalables dans la région on livré des informations de valeur, même si avec des grands hiatus. Un essai est présenté ici pour expliquer le statut changeant de la recherche prehistorique en Bengal, à l'aide de deux études de cas. Dans le premier – entrepris comme partie d'une dissertation de Doctorat – des sites microlithiques ont été étudiés avec une approche régionale. Une compréhension hlistique du comportement humain fut considérée à travers l'étude de la distribution des sites et l'analyse intensive des séquences de réduction. L'éthnographie fut utilisée pour une approche á des stratégies passées d'usage de la terre. Une approche multidisciplinaire fut addoptée pour l'étude du contexte qu'a livré des informations sur le paléoenvironment. Dans le second – en partie encore en cours – on est en train d'essayer de voir comment les perceptions passées du paysage peuvent être vues à partir de la distribution des sites microlithiques et de l'étude de leurs assemblages, plaçant ceci dans le cadre des études récéntes dans lesquels le paysage émerge comme phénomène culturelement construit. L'ethnographie est utilisée comme outil à diferents buts – pour voir à quel point elle peut apporter des approches aux perceptions passées.
Mots-clés: microlithique, processual, séquence de réduction, paysage, post-processuel, ethnographie, perception

The core region of Chotanagpur plateau comprising the modern state of Jharkhand, the south-eastern margins of the plateau or the western upland in West Bengal and northern Orissa have been extensively worked upon since the second half of the 19th century. Initiated by British geologists who made discoveries of 'chipped stones' and 'flakes' in the course of their mining surveys, prehistoric research in Bengal in the next century exposed the western upland (comprising Purulia and the western parts of Birbhum, Bankura, Burdwan and Midnapur) as a potential region for further studies (Basak 1998). We have traversed a long way since then in terms of changing perspectives in interpreting the archaeological record. Some lacunas are apparent in the earlier studies, which nevertheless form extremely valuable sources for information. I shall try to explain the changing status of prehistoric research in Bengal with the help of two case studies.

Tarafeni valley in north-west Midnapur was selected as part of a Ph.D dissertation (1992-1997) for a more holistic understanding of past human behaviour. By adopting a regional approach I undertook an intensive survey of microlithic sites, highlighting their nature, distribution variability and context of occurrence. Working within a functionalist processual framework I aimed at under-standing past strategies of land use adopted to cope with the environment. Thus instead of doing a stereotyped cataloguing of 'finished tools' I took the entire assemblage as a unit of analysis which threw light on processes of raw material procurement, manufacture, use, maintenance and discard of tools. I adopted a multi-disciplinary approach to study the context of the sites.

In my ongoing project (1999-) I am also dealing with microlithic scatters (in the region around Ayodhya hills, Purulia) from a slightly different perspective. Over the last decade or so landscape has emerged as a culturally constructed phenomenon, distinct from a landscape seen as a sum total of environmental features within a strictly ecological viewpoint.

Using microlithic scatters in Ayodhya hills as a case study I am trying to see how far perceptions of landscape can be seen from the locations of these scatters and a study of their assemblage. A rich, vibrant body of rituals, ceremonies, myths and symbolism surrounding the hills and other natural features in the landscape exists among the local indigenous communities. Using this as a tool to work with I am also trying to see how far ethnography can be used to offer insights into past perceptions. An archaeological study like this requires an essential prerequisite: - a systematic study of the context, which I have undertaken involving preliminary archaeological investigations.

Through these case studies I am trying to highlight the shifting perspectives in prehistoric studies in Bengal in the backdrop of contemporary advances in archaeological method and theory.

MICROLITHIC SITES IN THE TARAFENI VALLEY: A SUMMARY

Tarafeni valley (covering an area of 450 sq km: Fig. 4.1) in northwest Midnapore district was intensively surveyed over four field seasons. Forty-nine microlithic sites were located of which twenty-four were discovered by previous scholars. Instead of taking up isolated sites for investigation the distribution of both sites and scatters across the landscape was taken into account. Sites, here were defined as discrete clusters of artefacts occupying nodal points in the landscape, as distinguished from

occurrences of isolated artefact (s) or diffuse scatters ('off-site' or 'non-site') continuing between sites and distributed through out the landscape. A multidisciplinary approach was adopted to study the context of the sites that revealed new information on the late Quaternary palaeoenvironment and a chronology of Terminal Pleistocene was proposed (Basak 1997 a).

Preliminary geo-archaeological investigations of the stratigraphy indicated the prevalence of aridity in an overall sub-humid region. Fossil remains of certain deer species, buffalo etc. occurring at some of these sites suggested grassland vegetation agreeing well with the picture of aridity. Relative dating carried out on some of these fossil samples pointed to a time bracket of 18 000-10.000 BP, a period coinciding with the Terminal Pleistocene. Multi-disciplinary studies carried out in other regions in eastern India also indicate the prevalence of a cool, arid climate during the same period. A semi-arid environment in an otherwise sub-humid zone is indeed remarkable and this fits in very well with worldwide changes in the environment during the Last Glacial

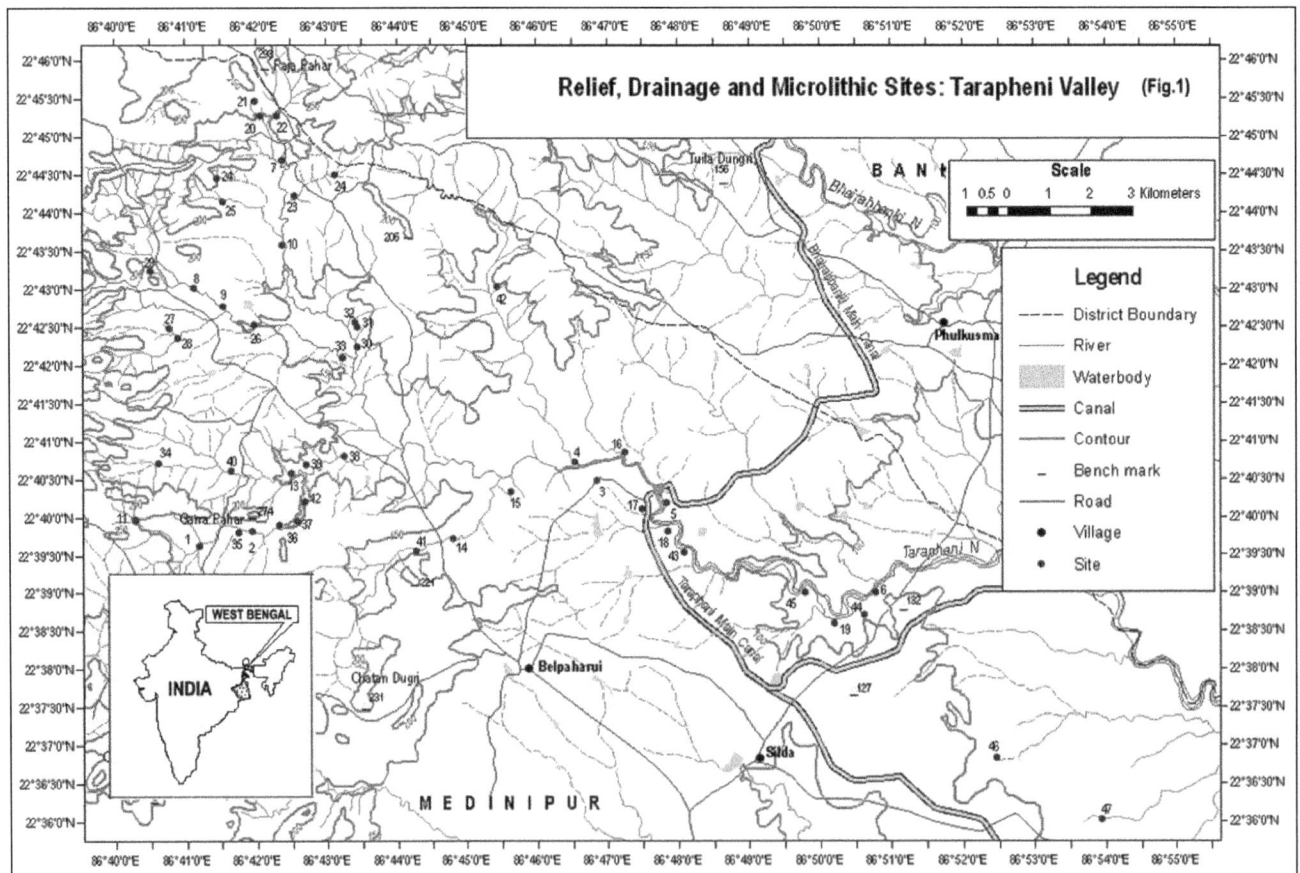

Fig. 4.1. Relief, Drainage and Microlithic Sites: Tarapheni Valley: 1. Kattara; 2. Aguibil 2; 3. Baishnabpur1; 4. Baishnabpur2; 5. Kurabhashapal; 6. Enthela; 7. Srinathpur; 8. Majigara; 9. Ashri 1; 10. Gidighati; 11. Benghuta; 12. Barighati 1; 13. Barighati 3; 14. Kalapathar; 15. Ghagra; 16. Jallangdih; 17. Bamundiha 1; 18. Balidanga; 19. Dhuliapur; 20. Dumohani; 21. Pataghar; 22. Barapal; 23. Kasijora; 24. Susnijobi; 25. Kandarbhula 1; 26. Kandarbhula 2; 27. Ashri2; 28. Adargaria 1; 29. Adargaria 1; 30. Joram; 31. Madhupur; 32. Charakpahari 1; 33. Charakpahari 2; 34. Amadubi; 35. Dongardihi; 36. Agubil 1; 37. Gohalberia 1; 38. Gohalberia 2; 39. Barighati 2; 40. Barighati 2; 41. Akuldoba; 42. Patpinra; 43. Pukhuria; 44. Bamundiha 2; 45. Gopalpur; 46. Rajdoha; 47. Kaliam; 48. Mohanpur

Maximum – prevalence of a cool, dry climate, lowering of sea level and spread of savanna and open woodland vegetation. (Basak 1997 a and c)

Studies in prehistory in India and particularly in Bengal usually look at stone tools as diagnostic forms of particular cultures and are thus reduced to a stereotyped cataloguing of "finished tools" followed by a technical analysis of the techniques of production. On the other hand, here, the entire assemblage was taken as the unit of analysis to see how the broad stages of reduction were reflected therein. The aim was to look at the processes of raw material procurement, manufacture, use, maintenance and discard of tools from the assemblage. These processes throw light on the past strategies and plans of land use adopted to cope with the environment in a particular context. This is known in archaeological literature as the study of "organization of technology" and is different from the study of a set of objects or "tools", an industry or a particular production technique that are the products of this adaptation. The methodology adopted here was built on similar studies of lithics carried out in other parts of the world. Ethnoarchaeological and ethnographic case studies of modern day hunter-gatherers were used as conceptual tools to gain an insight into past human behaviour.

Major sources of raw material used in the manufacture of the microliths were absent in the region. A few of these outcrops were located about 25-30 km west, north west of this region. Initial stages of trimming were also absent in the assemblages as seen from the nominal presence of cortical flakes and the negligible number of raw material blocks. The number of raw material blocks was very low as compared to the number of cores present. Thus it was surmised that on-place reduction of blade cores from nodules is non-existent in the region. Possibly partially made cores were brought here and the cortical flakes that were present formed bi-products of the post-initial trimming phase. Such evidences are prevalent in archaeological and ethnographic case studies. Subsequently, I tried to see how the post-initial trimming phase was reflected at the various sites, whether there was any difference in the way that different parts of the landscape were used in the past. Certain stretches of the landscape showed a greater concentration of sites. A differential discard of different artefact groups was also seen at different places. These parameters pointed to a differential place use. No definite answers were given as to why the region was important to prehistoric populations, only plausible reasons were suggested. Ultimately what emerged from this work was the diversity and complexity of human behavior and the myriad problems of defining them in material culture. (Basak 1997 b).

NEW VISTAS

In the past one decade or so landscape as a culturally constructed phenomenon has emerged as a distinctly important area in archaeological research, many of these ideas having been borrowed from social and cultural anthropology and cultural geography. Henceforth discussions on landscape crystallized into two polarized views: a previously-existing ecological one, which subsumed landscape under the broad rubric of environment to which human beings adapt; and a cultural one, which views landscape as 'meaningfully' constructed. Landscape became one of the important items of the processual/post-processual debate. A necessary component of the processual approach is a regional orientation to the archaeological record. A region is defined as a natural geographical unit with reference to one or more natural features. The relationship between people and landscape is seen as one of functional dependence along 'adaptive parameters' where issues like range of environmental resources exploited, resource-acquiring technologies, degree of mobility, seasonality and scheduling in relation to settlement size assumed supreme importance (Tilley 1994). Incidentally this is the approach that I had adopted while looking at past human behavior in Tarafeni valley.

Presently I am working within the perspective that landscape is a culturally constructed phenomenon (Ashmore and Knapp 1999). Through phenomenological approaches used by cultural and social anthropologists landscape has emerged as constituted by human dwelling, shaped by human choice and preferences. It follows from this that it is not universal and objective (Thomas 1993; Ashmore and Knapp 1999:14; Bender 1993). There are various readings of landscape, the result of different social and cultural contexts. Recent researches in ethnography and cultural anthropology have led to an 'unpacking' of the western idiom and encouraged one to look beyond an European construct. How people think and conceive their immediate 'space' and 'place' has become the central focus. Anthropological studies provide insights into the processes through which meanings and symbolisms grow around landscape. Archaeologists, while deviating from the traditional concept of 'site' have started looking more at natural places of significance in the landscape which yield residues of archaeological culture, and in doing so, they have drawn heavily on these studies.

Thus Landscape is not simply an aggregate of material resources as it was understood within a functionalist processual paradigm.

In a major work Tilley (1994)[1] argues that the landscape is suffused with myths, cosmologies and symbolisms which give an insight into how people perceive their environment. The same relief and drainage assume a different significance. Choice of particular locations for habitation or erection of monuments acquires a cultural meaning, as distinct from simple ecological connotation.

---

[1] There is voluminous literature on this, for initial readings see Bender (1993), Thomas (1993), Ashmore and Knapp (1999) and Bradley (2000).

This is not to dispute or disregard the importance of the latter. People do not occupy inhospitable locales only on the basis of a set of meanings and symbolisms. But with the passage of time the locales chosen for their habitational utility become associated with these meanings and symbolisms, which become too important to be ignored. As case studies Tilley selected one coastal and two inland regions in Wales and Dorset, distinctively different in relief from each other, which show a substantial presence of Mesolithic flint scatters and Neolithic monuments. Tilley argues that during the Mesolithic, in all three areas, ancestral connections between people and landscape were manifest in paths of movement and certain places along these paths assumed a particular significance to which they returned regularly in their seasonal activity rounds. However, these Mesolithic populations made very little impact on the land and what survives are some flint scatters. In the Neolithic the monuments restructured the relationship between people and landscape as it became more 'anchored'. Although differences existed among the three regions, the cultural memory of a 'place' and the connections between such many places were stabilized by the construction of monuments at these significant points. In a word, the landscape was 'appropriated'. Tilley relates this to subsistence practices and shows how these change from simple seasonal movements of animals in the Mesolithic to a more meaningful domestication in the Neolithic.

Such studies try to break landscape free from a dry environmental approach. However, for a holistic understanding of landscape an interdisciplinary approach is required, involving palaeo-ecology, environmental science, history, human geography, cultural anthropology and archaeology. Peoples' perceptions of land are extremely important, it is equally important to understand the palaeo-landscape, whether one is dealing with one landscape or more; the context of sites, whether they can be related to the same chronological period. This is all the more true for lithic scatters, a Neolithic or Megalithic monument on the other hand is more easily identifiable within a particular time frame.

In my ongoing project I am dealing with microlithic sites/scatters, in the region around Ayodhya hills, Purulia West Bengal. A discussion of this project will show how and to what extent it differs from my Ph. D dissertation.

LITHIC SCATTERS AND PERCEPTIONS OF LANDSCAPE: AYODHYA HILLS, PURULIA, WEST BENGAL

In Indian prehistory landscape has emerged in two ways - as a geographical region, providing the backdrop to a reconstruction of past life ways and as 'environment' where existing features are used to reconstruct the palaeo-environment. Landscape as a culturally constructed phenomenon has remained outside the boundary of these

studies. Unlike monuments, which have a more solid, anchored position in the landscape, lithic scatters are less 'impressionable'; therefore decoding their meanings and symbolism is more challenging and perhaps more difficult. Through my work I am trying to show that, despite limitations, stones do speak out to us. This has also been a personal journey through the landscape of Ayodhya hills, where sifting out a particular level of perception has been a complex task (Basak 2005).

TOPOGRAPHY, LOCATION AND THE CONTEXT OF SITES

Purulia, the western-most district of West Bengal, is topographically dominated by a hilly western part with an elevation of 300-600 m and an open eastern upland of 150-300 m. The highlands are marked by a principal knot of hills called the Ajodhya hills (Fig. 4.2). To the immediate east and south of this integrated mass are a few extended hills which extend as spurs from the parent body. These are the Budha-ar (557 m), the Kanapahar (453 m) and the Matha-buru (665 m). In some places, as near Budha-ar and Kanapahar jumbled masses of weathered granite and gneiss are seen, resting at the foothills. Some of these are also seen to rest at the top. The hills act as a watershed between the Kasai and the Subarnarekha rivers. Numerous small streams drain the western and the southern slopes before meeting Subarnarekha, and the northern and eastern slopes before meeting the Kasai and the Kumari. These tributaries are again fed by many feeder channels forming their catchment area. To the north, west and south of the Ajodhya hills occur a number of residual hills, isolated and detached from the parent body as in and around Jhalda in the north and north west and in the Bandowan-Kuilapal area in the south east. All these hills are an extension of the hills in Ranchi, Singhbhum and Hazaribagh, thus forming a part of the fringe area of Chotanagpur in Bengal.

A pattern of distribution of sites/scatters emerged from the first two seasons of fieldwork (Basak 2001 a and b). 24 sites/scatters were located in an area of 84 sq km. These were mostly located in the foothills of the isolated hills of Budha-ar, the Kanapahar and Chauniya, which form the Tor landscape. A fourth concentration of sites was located in the headwaters of Kumari near Kerwa village. All these sites are characterized by rocky outcrops and boulders standing erect. A few isolated sites/scatters were marked out, away from these principal zones of concentration.

The principal raw material used in the manufacture of these microliths was a black chert which is often accruing a grey, white or a yellowish patina. A small fraction of quartz is present along with a few specimens of jasper, chalcedony and a particular variety of quartzite. None of the outcrops are present at the sites or in their vicinity. Outcrops of chert were traced at Dubrajpur and the

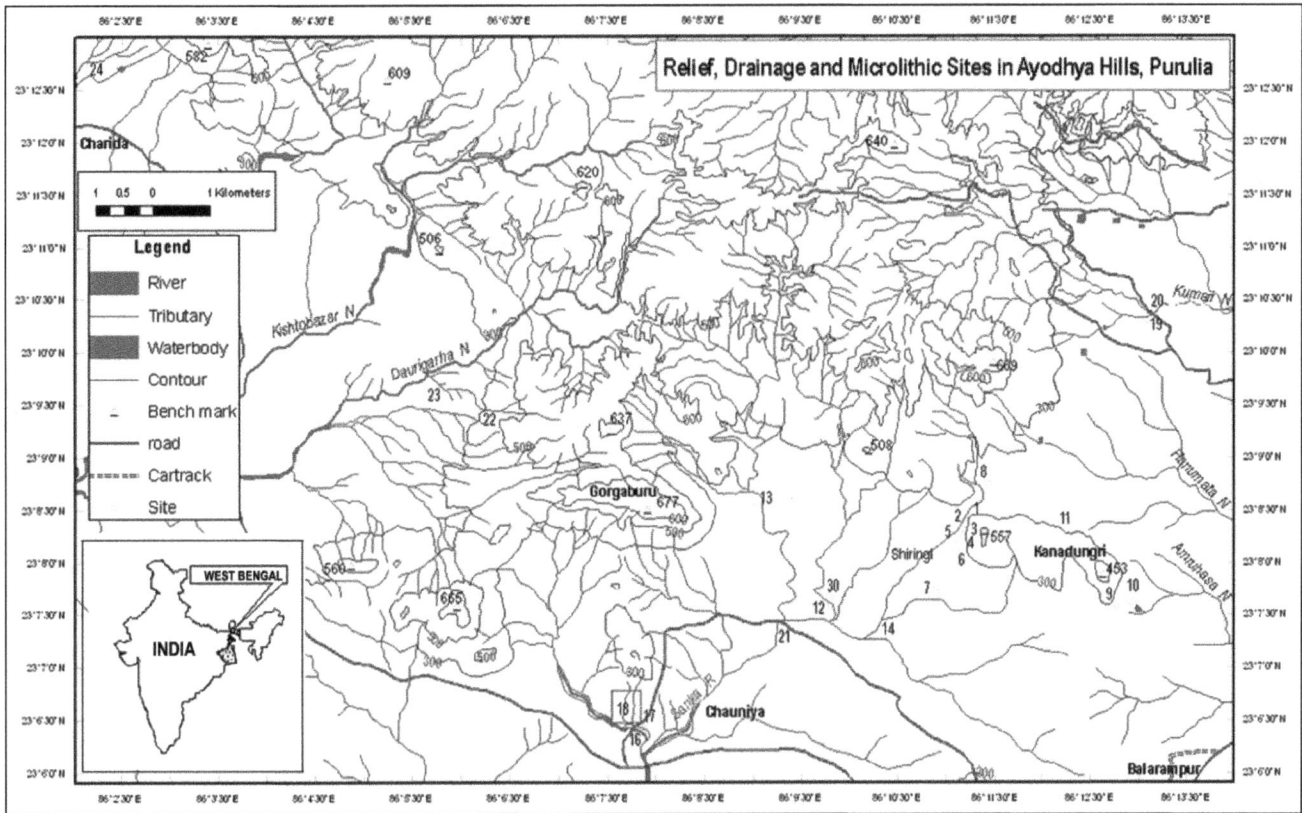

Fig. 4.2. Relief, Drainage and Microlithic Sites in Ayodhya Hills, Purulia: 1. Siringi 1; 2. Siringi 2; 3. Siringi 3; 4. Siringi 4; 5. Siringi 5; 6. Siringi 6; 7. Digdih; 8. Bersa; 9. Kana1 & Kana2; 10. Kana3; 11. Purabbad; 12. Garga; 13. Badhna; 14. Nekra-Gopalpur; 17. Mathaburu; 18. Chauniya 1; 19. Chauniya 2; 20. Chauniya 3; 24. Kerwa1; 25. Kerwa2; 26. Nekre; 27. Sukridoba 1; 28. Sukridoba 2; 29. Rabidih

adjoining region, 4-8 km east of Chandil in Jharkhand, approximately 30 km south/southeast of the area of study.

Preliminary geoarchaeological investigations revealed that all the sites are associated with a colluvial context, overlain by an oxisol and underlain by a reddish silt. The stratigraphy bears a striking resemblance to that seen in the Tarafeni valley. Hence on the basis of these observations the sites/scatters in the Ayodhya region have been approximately assigned to the Terminal Pleistocene (Basak 2001 a and b). A methodology similar to the one adopted for the earlier project was followed to study the lithic assemblage. The initial stage of reduction is conspicuous by its absence as seen from the absence of raw material blocks, less proportion of decortification flakes and rough outs, characteristics of that stage. Early stages of reduction following manufacture are only nominally present at some sites, otherwise all the sites are marked by late stages of reduction, represented by cores, mostly abandoned after a heavy use, a few trimmed nodules utilized to extract blades, a small proportion of blade and blade tools, different categories of flakes in varying proportions and other post manufacturing debris. These activities are mainly restricted to the four loci of concentration of sites in the foothill region of the isolated hills. Small sites/scatters and diffused occurrences,

located away from these hills were only ephemerally utilized (Basak 2001 a and b).

Thus these hills or rather their foothill region and the rocky outcrops appear to be the nodal points of human activity. The hills by their towering presence evoke a sense of awe; the rocky outcrops are natural markers in the landscape. Over time they have accrued a rich body of legends, myths and stories, the hills are also the sacred sites of some annual rituals. This clearly emerges from an ethnographic survey of two principal festivals - one is held on the first day of the Bengali month *magh* (January) when the hills or the deities believed to be living in these hills are venerated and another locally known as the *Baha parab* is held in the month of *Falgun* (corresponding to February-March) when the entire landscape is venerated, celebrating the first full moon of the month and the first blossoming of *Sal* (*Shorea robusta*). On the night of *purnima* or the full moon in the month of *Baishakh* (April-May) the Ayodhya hill becomes the focal point of an annual hunt (*Disum sendra),* a ritual maintained in the face of dwindling forests and wild life. (see Basak 2005 for a discussion of these ceremonies). Principally held among the local tribal communities these are times of congregation for people often coming from far-flung places, cementing ties of kinship and solidarity. Such means of ascribing meaning to the landscape are not uncommon especially among the indigenous people. In fact archaeologists and anthropologists working on landscape believe there are certain physical landscapes with outstanding natural features, which are considered to be special/sacred to all, irrespective of one's cultural background (Tacon 1999: 34; Bradley 2000). Among the Australian aborigines the entire landscape is conceived to be a mosaic of dream tracks where every natural feature becomes an embodiment of symbolism through myths and ceremonies. Among others like the Wamirians and the Apaches every part of the landscape is redolent with myths and symbolisms (see Basak 2005 for a discussion on this).

In trying to understand past perceptions I am not suggesting any unbroken continuity of rituals and ceremonies between the past and the present. In fact the memory of these traditions goes back to only 500 years, as revealed by my ethnographic queries. What emerges as important in Ayodhya is the significance ascribed to these natural markers in the landscape. The location of sites and scatters around these natural markers assumes a new meaning in this light. Visually significant these natural markers may have acted as nodes of congregation to highly mobile populations returning to these places more than once, the latter becoming places of substantial activity, used intensively over a short time/long period or both. The 'less significant' scatters located away from these nodes may have been ephemerally utilized as seen from their assemblage. However this may not diminish their significance as places. Tuan (1977) argues that many deeply loved places are not visible at all.

This is a shift from a functionalist approach of landscape followed in the earlier project where the emphasis was chiefly on understanding past strategies of use and reuse of landscape from the lithic record.

Acknowledgements

I would personally like to thank Sutapa Roy, Centre for Archaeological Studies and Training, Eastern India, Kolkata, India for the maps.

References

ASHMORE, W. and A.B. KNAPP 1999. Archaeologies of Landscape, Contemporary Perspectives. Oxford: Blackwell.

BASAK, B. 1997 a. Prehistoric Settlement Patterns in Tarafeni Valley, Midnapur district West Bengal: Thesis submitted to the University for Poona for doctoral degree.

BASAK, B. 1997 b. 'Microlithic sites in the Tarafeni valley, Midnapur district, West Bengal: A Discussion' *Man and Environment* 22 (2): 11-28.

BASAK, B. 1997 c. 'Late Quaternary Environment, Palaeontology and Culture in Tarafeni valley, Midnapur, West Bengal - A Preliminary Study' *Jour. of Geo. Soc. of India* 51:731-740.

BASAK, B. 1998. 'Microlithic sites in the Kharsoti and Subarnarekha valleys: some observations and comments' *Pratnasamiksha* 3&4:1-19.

BASAK, B. 2001a. 'Microlithic sites in the Western upland of Purulia: A holistic study (Phase I: The Ayodhya Hills)', *Pratnasamikhsha* 6&8: 1-28.

BASAK, B. 2001b. Microlithic sites in the Western upland of Purulia (Phase II: The Ayodhya Hills), Occasional paper 12.Centre for Archaeological Studies and Training, eastern India, Kolkata.

BASAK, B. 2005 'Perceiving the landscape: lithic scatters in Ayodhya hills, Purulia', *Man and Environment*, XXX(2): 12-23.

BENDER, B. 1993. Landscape: Politics and Perspectives. Oxford: Berg.

BRADLEY, R. 2000. An Archaeology of Natural Places. London: Routledge.

TACON, P.S.C. 1999. Identifying Ancient Sacred Landscape in Australia: From Physical to Social, in Archaeologies of Landscape, Contemporary Perspectives (W. Ashmore and A.B. Knapp Eds), pp. 33-57. Oxford: Blackwell.

THOMAS, J. 1993. The Politics of Vision and the Archaeologies of Landscape, in Landscape: Politics and Perspectives (B. Bender ed.) pp. 19-48. Oxford: Berg.

TILLEY, C.1994. A Phenomenology of Landscape: Places, Paths and Monuments. Oxford: Berg.

TUAN Y. 1977. Space and Place: The Perspective of Experience. Minneapolis: University of Minnesota Press.

THE NEOLITHIC CULTURE IN THE NORTHERN VINDHYAS AND THE MIDDLE GANGETIC PLAIN

J.N. PAL

Department of Ancient history, Culture and archaeology, University of Allahabad, India

Abstract: The archaeological excavations in northern Vindhyas and the middle Gangetic plains have revealed the evidence of first farming culture going back to 6th-5th millennium B.C. The culture is marked by hand made ceramic industries (characteristic feature being the cord impressed pottery), microliths, ground and polished Neolithic celts, bone tools, domesticated and wild animal bones and cultivated and wild plant remains. The area has emerged as one of the earliest centers of rice cultivation. The Neolithic settlements are marked by hut floors. We propose to present the status of this first farming culture of northern India as revealed from recent excavations especially at Tokwa, Jhusi, Hetapatti, Lahuradeva, etc.
Keywords: India; Neolithic; Ganga Palin; Vindhyas; Ceramic Industry, Chronology; Microliths

Résumé: Les fouilles archéologiques au Vindhyas du Nord et le plaines moyennes du Gangetic ont révélé l'évidence de la première culture paysanne datant du 6ème-5ème milénaire A.C. La culture est marquée par la présence de céramiques manuelles (les impréssions cordées étant le trait caractéristique), de microlithes, de la pierre polie, des outils en os, des ossements d'animaux doméstiqués et sauvages, ainsi que des restes domestiqués et sauvages de plantes. L'aire a émergé comme un des ppremiers centres de cultivation du riz. Les sites néolithiques sont définis par de fonds de cabannes. On se propose de pésenter le status de cette première culture paysanne du nord de l'Inde, tel qu'elle fut révélée par des fouilles récentes à Tokwa, Jhusi, Hetapatti, Lahuradeva, etc.
Mots-clés: Inde, Néolithique, Ganga Palin, Vindhyas, industrie céramique, cronologie, microlithes

INTRODUCTION

The northern Vindhyas and the middle Gangetic plain, situated in north-central India constitute two contrasting ecological and geographical zones – one rocky plateau of Bundelkhand and Baghelkand in the south and the flat alluvial plain of the ganga in the north. Vindhyan region lying south of the Gangetic plain is marked by diverse topographical features. It is generally hilly and characterized by step formation gradually rising from north-east to south-west marked by rugged and diverse topography. The region is made of granite-gneiss, sand stone, shale and serrated ridges of quartz reefs. The north central Vindhyan region has been one of the most, archaeologically investigated areas of India, which was geomorphologically and ecologically an ideal region for the origin and development of the human cultures, where antiquity of human cultures goes back to the middle Pleistocene period. Evidence of Palaeolithic, Mesolithic, Neolithic, Chalcolithic cultures along with transitional and transformational phases is very significant to understand the developmental process of the cultures. The longest Quaternary geological and cultural sequence has been worked out in the valleys of the Belan and the Son. Geological formations have documented the climatic and environmental changes during the Pleistocene and early Holocene periods. A large number of sites ranging in age from Lower Palaeolithic to early historic have been located and a good number of them have been put to excavation. Palaeontological, palaeobotanical and palaeozoological studies conducted by multidiscipline research teams of scholars of Allahabad University and other national and international institutions have furnished valuable data to reconstruct the developmental process of the human cultures.

The Ganga Plain, lying between Himalayan Tarai in the north and the Vindhyas in the south is divisible into three main units: (i) Upper Ganga Plain, (ii) Middle Ganga Plain, and (iii) Lower Ganga Plain. It is a flat alluvial land, marked by rivers originating from the Himalayas, horse-shoe-lakes and rivulets emerging from these lakes and has a slope from north west to south east. The middle Gangetic plain measuring about 144.409 sq. km, is bounded by the Ganga-Yamuna confluence in the west and Bihar-Bengal border in the east. It includes modern eastern Uttar Pradesh and plain of Bihar. From the point of view of origin and development of human cultures in the plain the middle Ganga plain is most significant. It has been the cradle of Indian civilization right from the terminal Pleistocene period. Archaeological investigations conducted during last four decades by University of Allahabad, Banaras Hindu University, Deen Dayal Upadhyaya University Gorakhpur, University of Patna, U.P. State Archaeology Department, Bihar State Archaeology Department and Archaeological Survey of India, Patna Circle have furnished a complete cultural sequence of the region – Epipalaeolithic, Mesolithic, Neolithic, Chalcolithic, Early Iron Age and historical periods. Right from the earliest phase, i.e. Epiplaeolithic and Mesolithis both regions have been in close cultural contacts. The Gangetic plain was far the first time colonized by the Stone Age culture of the Vindhyas. We propose to present the status of this first farming culture of northern India as revealed from recent excavations especially at Tokwa, Jhusi, Hetapatti, Lahuradeva, etc. (Fig. 5.1)

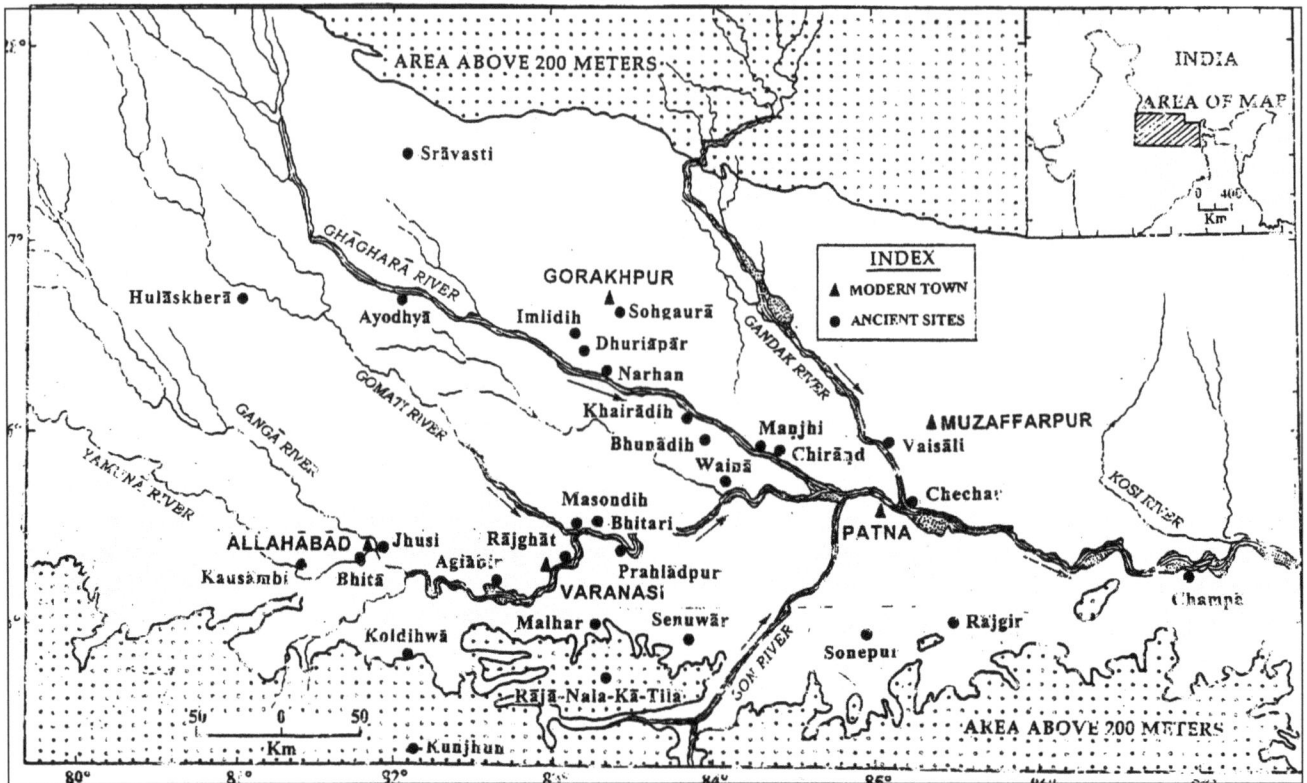

Fig. 5.1. Excavated Archaeological Sites in the Ganga Plain

NEOLITHIC IN THE NORTH-CENTRAL VINDHYAS

Though the discovery of first recognized finds of the Neolithic celts in India was made by Le Mesurier (1861: 81-85) as early as 1860 in the Tons valley of the north-central Vindhyas, but the discovery of Neolithic implements in archaeological context in the region is almost a recent event, being unearthed from the excavations at Koldihwa in 1972-73 (Misra 1977: 107-121, Misra 2006). Neolithic celts fashioned on basalt had been collected from the hilly tracts of Lalitpur, Hamirpur, Banda, Allahabad and Mirzapur districts from time to time (Allchin and Allchin 1968: 172). Triangular celts, conforming to the characteristic tools types of South Indian Neolithic groups was the main tool type discovered in the area. Besides, a few rounded celts supposed to be characteristic tool type of the Neolithic culture of North-East India and further a field of South-East Asia were also met with. The distribution of the these two types of celts shos that in the eastern part of the region rounded celts were in profusion, while the triangular celts were found in the western parts.

Besides Koldihwa the round celts have been obtained in course of excavations in a definite archaeological context from Mahagara and Panchoh (Sharma *et.al.* 1980: 135-36) in the Belan Valley in Allahabad district on the one hand and from Indari (*IAR 1980-81*: 71), and Tokwa (Misra *et.al.* 2000: 45-57; Misra *et.al.* 2000-2001; 59-72) in the Adwa Valley in the Mirzapur district of U.P. and

from the Kunjhun (*IAR 1981-82*: 43-44, Clark and Khanna 1989) on the Son in Sidhi district of M.P., its high antiquity is suggested both by its archaeological context and C^{14} dates. In this connection it may be pointed out that none of the excavated sites mentioned above has yielded triangular celts so far. A greater antiquity to the rounded celt tradition in comparison to the triangular celt tradition is suggested in the northern Vindhyas.

The excavations at Koldhiwa presented a distinct personality of the Neolithic culture of the northern Vindhyas. A planned and persistent archaeological investigations carried out in the area roughly bounded in the north by the Ganga and in the south by the Son over decades by the Department of Ancient History, Culture and Archaeology, University of Allahabad brought to light a good number of sites associated with rounded celts. Of the important sites mentioned may be made of Koldihwa, Mahagara, Panchoh, Kukrahta, Deoghat, Koilariha, Futahawa, Chaurdih-Kotia, Bansghat, Daiya and Patehari (Pal 1986: 36-38) in the Belan Valley in Allahabad district; Magha, Indari, Beraundha, Sinduria, Mahalpur and Tokwa in the Adwa Valley in Mirzapur district, and Kunjhun, Lalnahia, and Dhobauhi in Sidhi district of M.P. (Pal 1986: 36-38). Of these, Koldihwa (Misra 1977: 107-19), Mahagara (Sharma *et.al.* 1980: 133-200), Panchoh (IAR 1975-76: 47), Indari (*IAR 1980-81*: 72), Tokwa (Misra *et.al.* 2001: 59-72) and Kunjhun (Clark and Khanna 1989, *IAR 1981-82*: 43-44) have been excavated.

Tokwa (Lat. 24o 54′ 20″ N., Long. 82o 16′ 45″ E.) the important archaeological site, is situated at an elevation of 146 m MSL on the confluence of the Belan and Adwa in Lalganj sub-division of Mirzapur District of Uttar Pradesh, at a distance of 68 km from Mirzapur city in south eastern direction and at a distance of 8 km east of Baraundha. Excavations conducted at the site during 2000 (Misra *et al.* 2000-2001, 2001) and 2002 have revealed cultural relics of Neolithic, Chalcolithic and Early Iron Age periods. Of the sites associated with Vindhyan Neolithic, excavated/explored so far, Tokwa appears to be most extensive and well preserved. From excavation at Tokwa it appears that there was a gap between the disappearance of the Neolithic culture and arrival of the Chalcolithic culture as these two cultures exhibit different trades in ceramic tradition. While Neolithic pottery is hand made the Chalcolithic is wheel thrown.

The excavations at the sites have revealed several aspects of the Neolithic culture of the northern Vindhyas:

Settlement Pattern: Neolithic settlements have been located on the banks of rivers or nalas, generally above the flood plain. Neighbouring flood plains provided fertile fields for agriculture by annual inundations, which could be cultivated without tilling and irrigation. These are sedentary settlements, generally situated in shallow basin-shaped bluff surrounded by natural ridges. The ridge played the role of defense walls against flood, cold winds, and wild animals. As the evidence shows, the Neolithic people were not dependent on agriculture alone for their subsistence. They domesticated animals and exploited wild plants and animals in the nearby forests, rich in woodland and grassland vegetation. The rivers and nalas not only provided suitable land for agriculture, they also provided food in the form of aquatic animals like fish, tortoise, snail, etc.

Structures: The evidence of structures has been found in the form of hut floors and cattlepen from the excavation at Mahagara. On the other excavated sites the structural evidence is very poor mainly due to limited area of excavation and disturbance of Neolithic strata by later activities. However, the burnt clay lumps with wattle and daub impressions obtained in profusion from all the habitation sites indicate that thatched huts were prepared by bamboo and wooden posts and mud-plastered screen walls. Traces of a hut floor were also observed at Indari during excavation. As is evident from the excavations from Mahagara, there appears a pattern in the layout of hutment. All the 18 hut floors exposed at the site are circular or oval on plan. The area covered by huts varies from 6.70x6.25 m to 5.0x3.50 m. The average living area in a hut is 15.74 sq. m. The floors are surrounded by postholes, varying from 6 to 9 in number, on their periphery. The posts supported the upper roof as well as the side screen wall. Oval or round hut floors encircled by postholes were also exposed at Neolithic Tokwa.

The cattle pen exposed at Mahagara is one of the most remarkable discoveries of structures. The cattle pen, located in the south-east sector of the site is irregular rectangular on plan and measures 12.5 m in length and 7.5. m. in width. It was surrounded by four houses on its four corners so that it could be constantly watched against attack by wild animals. Having three openings, two to the east and one to the west, the cattle pen was enclosed by thatched screen walls as is evident by the discovery of 28 postholes around the pen. As there is no evidence of postholes inside the pen, it may be suggested that the pen was open to sky and the cattle were put inside it untied. At least 23 pairs of hoof imprints of cattle of different age groups have been located within the pen.

Subsistence: The subsistence of the Neolithic people was based on the exploitation of plants and animals, by domestication as well as by hunting and gathering. The evidence of cultivation of plants has been found in the form of rice husk used as degraissant in the pottery as well as charred grains of rice of domesticated variety. The presence of a wild variety of rice along with a domesticated variety is significant which presents the practice of collecting wild rice along with cultivation of rice. The cultivated variety of rice has been identified as *Oryza sativa* and wild variety are annual and perennial *Oryza nivara* and *Oryza rufigona*. (Vishnu-Mittre and Sharma n.d.). The wild variety of rice was also present in the last phase of the Mesolithic culture at Chopani Mando. Imprints of *Ischaemum rugosum* also have been identified from Mahagara which is a common weed grown in marshy paddy fields. Recent studies of the botanical remains from Koldihwa and mahagara by Emma Harvey and Dorian Fuller have thrown welcome light on the range of cereals cultivated by the Neolithic people of the northern Vindhyas. Crops identified at Koldihwa and Mahagara include rice, barley, wheat, pulses, sesame and small millets. That wild grain was a part of the diet of the Neolithic people is also attested by the finding of millet-like grains from Koldihwa. The available evidence suggests that wild and cultivated variety of rice and millets were used from the beginning of the Neolithic settlements at Koldiwa and mahagara and barley, wheat, pulses and sesame were introduced subsequently. K.S. Saraswat has come to similar conclusion at Tokwa, where Neolithic people were cultivating rice and millet in the beginning and with the passage of time they also started cultivating barley, wheat, green gram, lentil, etc. (Misra n.d.). Other botanical remains recovered from excavations include charred seeds of jujube and charred bamboo fragments.

A large number of animal bones have been collected from the excavation at Mahagara, Koldihwa and Kunjhun. They included both domesticated as well as wild species. The domesticated animals have been identified by Alur (1980) as cattle (*Bos indicus*), sheep/goat, and wild ones such as deer (*Cervidae*), antelope, boar (*Sus scrofa*) and horse (*Equidae*). The animal bones recovered from Kunjhun include cattle, deer, antelope and dog. A good number of bones of tortoise, fish and bird also have been found from almost all the excavated sites, and these supplemented the diet of Neolithic people.

Material Culture: The artefacts recovered from the habitation sites give ample evidence of the life pattern of the first farming communities of the Vindhyas. Recording of the artefacts distributed on the hut floors presents some indication about some specialized craftsmanship connected with some huts. The artefacts connected with food-producing, food processing and hunting-gathering include celts, querns, mullers, bored stones, microliths, bone tools, pottery, etc.

The querns, mullers, sharpeners, rubber stones, hammers, anvils, stone discs, sling balls and bored stones, most of which were food processing equipment, are made of sand stone or quartzite. The querns morphologically are divisible into two groups: (I) basin-shaped and (ii) flat. Basin-shaped querns are heavily used. There are ample circular marks on the slope of the basin-shaped querns indicating that the upper grinding stone was used rotating on the quern. The mullers are marked with pitted surface and have unifaced or multifaced working surface. Most of the stone objects have been fashioned by pecking and grinding. Some of the hammers, anvils and sling balls also have evidence of pitted surface on their working edges. The sharpeners and rubber stones have heavily rubbed use-marks. The bored stones with hour-glass perforation also have been made by pecking and grinding.

The microlithic industry is an integral part of the Neolithic cultural assemblage. Chalcedony, chert, agate, carnelian and quartz and crystal were the raw material for manufacturing microliths. The microlithic artefacts may broadly be divided into two groups: (i) waste material and (ii) tools. The waste material includes cores, flakes and chips. The tools on typo-technological considerations have been grouped into retouched blades, backed blades, backed and truncated blades, serrated blades, points, awls, trapezes, lunates and tranchets. Some of the blades having shining gloss on their working edges presumably due to use for cutting green vegetation. There are a good number of large-sized flakes made of grey chert, some of which have use marks on their edges. Having a sharp working edge, these flakes possibly played the role of heavy duty tools and were used for cutting and scraping.

Single tanged bone arrowheads marked with pointed end are the tools other than microliths used in hunting by the Neolithic people. The evidence of bone tools is available from Tokwa and Mahagara.

Ceramic industry is one of the most diagnostic traits of the Neolithic culture of the northern Vindhyas. Statistically also it is the richest among the cultural assemblages. It is a hand made pottery. On the basis of surface treatment the ceramic industry has been divided into four major groups: (i) Cord-impressed ware (ii) Rusticated ware (iii) Burnished red ware and (iv) Burnished black ware (Pal 1986).

The clay used for shaping the pottery is not well levigated and it contains calcium granules and small iron nodules. Husk of rice and millet, chopped straw and leaves and cow-dung have been mixed as degraissant in the clay. The pottery is hand made as is evident by palm and finger impressions on both sides of the uneven pot surfaces. The fabric varies from coarse to medium. The surface colour of first two groups is generally matt red and those of third and fourth groups are bright red and black respectively. The core colour of the pots is smoky grey to blackish due to organic temper mixed in the clay and ill-firing.

The functional pottery types are very simple but to some extent standardized. These include convex, straight or tapering sided deep and shallow bowls; tubular spouted bowls; straight, concave or carinated necked jars; basins, handis and platters. The carinated neck of jars and the tubular spouts were luted to the jars and bowls respectively made separately. The decoration of pottery is confined only to applique and incised designs.

The pots were provided cord-impressed decorative pattern when the pots were leather hard. An experiment on the manufacturing technique of the cord-impressed ware shows that cord impressed pattern can be obtained by using tortoise bones as dabber and thus the ware may be termed as tortoise bone impressed ware (Pal 1987). However, the employment of cord-wrapped paddle for imparting the cording pattern on some of the pots can not be totally ruled out. The cord-impressed pattern varies from thick to thin and deep to indistinct. The cording strokes are vertical, horizontal, oblique, slanting and occasionally multidirectional.

The rusticated ware is marked by roughened external surface of the pots. The rustication has been done by clay solution mixed with husk, chopped leaves and straw, grits and calcium granules. The rustication was done, possibly, to make the pots more sturdy and hardened. Sometimes pots of cord impressed ware and burnished red ware also have been rusticated.

The burnished red ware is characterized by a bright red ochrous slip and burnishing. The bowls have been slipped and burnished on both the surfaces while the jars have this treatment only on outer surface.

The burnished black ware marked by black slip and burnishing has same features, techno-typologically, as those of the burnished red ware.

The other artefacts associated with the Neolithic culture of the Vindhyas include pottery disc with central perforation (made of potsherds, possibly used as whorl for spinning), terracotta dabber, spherical beads of terracotta and shell pendant.

NEOLITHIC IN THE MIDDLE GANGA PLAIN

As mentioned earlier the archaeological investigations carried in the middle Ganga plain have revealed evidence of the Stone Age relating to the Epipalaeolithic and Mesolithic cultures. In the western part of the middle Ganga valley, where a good number of preceding Mesolithic sites are located, the succeeding Neolithic culture was not present before the discovery of Neolithic settlement at Jhusi (Misra *et al.* 2004) and Hetapatti (Pal and Gupta 2005) in Allahabad district.

Jhusi (Lat. 250 26′ 10″ N., Long. 810 54′ 30″ E.), the ancient Pratisthanpur, is located on the left bank of the Ganga within a marked meander very close to the Ganga-Yamuna confluence at a distance of about 7 km to the east of Allahabad city. The Department of Ancient History, Culture and Archaeology, University of Allahabad has conducted excavations at the site on Samudrakup mound for five seasons, 1995 (Misra *et al.* 1995-96), 1998 (Misra *et al.* 1998-99), 1999 (Misra *et al.* 1999-2000), 2002 (Misra *et al.* 2002-2003) and 2003 (Gupta and Pal 2004) in four areas. It is a multi-culture site having occupational deposit of the Neolithic culture at the base.

A new site of the Neolithic culture at Hetapatti (Lat. 25.49386° N., Long. 81.91686° E.) is located on the left bank of the Ganga. It is at a distance of about 20 km from Allahabad in north-east direction, and is being excavated by the Department of ancient History, Culture and Archaeology, University of Allahabad (Pal and Gupta 2005). The identification of Neolithic level at Jhusi and Hetapatti in Allahabad on the Ganga presents for the first time Neolithic culture on the western margin of mid Ganga plain. There may be hidden Neolithic settlements in between the eastern and western margin of the area.

The explorations conducted in the eastern part of the mid Ganga valley during the last four decades have resulted in identifying several Neolithic settlements in this region. The important excavated sites in Uttar Pradesh other than Jhusi and Hetapatti of Allahabad, include Bhunadih (Singh and Singh 1997-98) and Waina (Singh and Singh 1995-96) in Ballia, Sohgaura (*IAR 1974-75*: 46-47, Chatur-vedi 1985) and Imlidih Khurd (Singh 1992-93, 1993-94; Singh *et al.* 2003, 2004-2005) in Sant Kabirnagar, while Chirand (*IAR 1981-82*: 13-14,Verma 1971, Narain 1970, Varma 1998, Sinha 1994, Roy 1989) in Saran, Chechar Kutubpur (*IAR 1977-78*: 17-18) in Vaisali, Taradih (*IAR 1984-85*: 9-10) in Gaya and Senuwar (Singh 1990, 1997, 2004) in Rohtas in Bihar. Most of these excavated sites are multi-culture sites having yielded archaeological relics ranging from Neolithic to early historical periods.

Settlement Pattern: All the excavated sites are located on the banks of rivers, generally on the confluence of two rivers near meander above the flood plain or on horse-shoe lakes (as in the case of Lahuradeva). The size of total settlement is moderate. The thickness of the occupational strata ranges from 45-50 cm to about 2m.

Structures: The excavations, though conducted on a limited scale, have brought to light evidence of circular or oval huts known through the patterns of post-holes that have come to light from almost all excavated sites of the area. Wattle and daub structure is attested by good number of burnt clay with reed and bamboo impression. At Chirand, the evidence of pit dwelling has also been reported. Of the other structural remains mention may be made of hearths, pits and silo probably for storing grains.

Subsistence: The Neolithic people of the Ganga valley as those of the Vindhyas were farming and pastoral communities is attested by the cultivated variety of barley, wheat, rice, field pea, lentil, green gram, etc. recovered from the excavated sites. However, the botanical evidence obtained from Senuwar and Jhusi in mid Ganga valley read with its counter part of Tokwa in the Vindhays suggests that in the early phase only rice and some primitive millets were being cultivated. With the passage of time other cereals were also added to the corpus of cultivated variety. The Neolithic deposit at Senuwar (Singh 2001: 109-118) is divided into two subgroups 1A and 1B. From the lowest part of the middle of period IA only grains of cultivated rice, (*Oryza sativa*) were found along with wild plants like jobs tear, fox tail/bandra, wild rice, *jharberi*, *chaulai* and wild *palaka*. But in the later phase of IA new cereals like barley, wheat, *jowar* millet, lentil, field pea, finger millet (*ragi*) and *khesari* were introduced. The available evidence is demonstrative of the fact that by the late phase of Neolithic culture in the mid Ganga valley, double crop pattern had become an accomplished fact.

Domesticated animals include cattle, buffalo, sheep, goat and pigs. Besides these, the bones of elephants, rhinoceros, stag, deer, etc. have also been found from some of the sites. Of aquatic fauna whose bones have been found, mention may be made of fish and turtle. Bones of birds have also been found. The available evidence, thus, indicates that besides agriculture and domestication the Neolithic people of the mid Ganga plain also practiced hunting, catching and fishing.

Material Culture: The ceramic industry of the Neolithic Gangetic plain is rich and varied. The available evidence indicates that in the early stage of the culture, as indicated at Chirand, Lahuradeva, Jhusi and Hetapatti, people were using hand made pottery but subsequently the slow wheel appears to have been used for the purpose. The ceramic assemblage includes ordinary red ware, lustrous red ware, burnished ware (red, black and grey), rusticated ware, black-and-red ware and corded ware. The clay used for manufacturing the pots is not well levigated. It contains grits, husks and chaff as degraissant. Pots are generally ill fired and have blackish grey core. Pottery types exhibit variety suggesting thereby that these were put to different uses. Pottery types include bowls with varying profile, vases, vessels, basins, miniature jars, *handis*, etc. Bowls basins and vases also have some times spouts. The cording exhibits dozen of patterns. Some of the pots, generally vases, were made in two parts separately- the lower portion and the rim portion and subsequently these were luted together. Occurrence of painted sherds has been reported from Imlidih Khurd, Lahuradeva, Chirand and Senuwar. The post firing paintings of Chirand and Senuwar are confined to the rim and have been executed in red ochre. At Chirand the painting motifs consist of linear designs of criss-cross lines and concentric circles. At Imlidih Khurd painting executed in white red pigment over a bright slip has been reported. Post firing scratching by sharp instrument is another feature of decorating the pots. Often the scratching results in geometric patterns such as opposed triangles within concentric circles and floral motifs. Pots with appliqué bands have also been reported. On these appliqué are executed chain and rope patterns or incised decorations. In this connection it may be pointed out that appliqué patterns are confined to big pots like *handis* and basins. Wheel-thrown pots are reported from the late Neolithic phase of Senuwar.

As revealed from the excavated sites the culture is associated with microlithic industry. Bladelets, flakes, blades, scrapers, arrowheads, serrated points, lunates, borers, etc. fashioned on chert, chalcedony, agate, jasper, and quartz have been found from some of the sites. However, celts of basalt and granite have been obtained from Lahuradeva, Chirand and Senuwar. Heavy duty stone objects include fragments of querns, mullers, balls, hammer stones, etc., fashioned on sandstone or quartzite. Beads, finished and unfinished and fashioned on chalcedony, agate, etc. have been found at Jhusi, Chirand and Senuwar. Chirand, Lahuradeva, Jhusi and Hetapatti have also yielded beads of steatite and/or faience.

Bone tools have been found at Jhusi, Senuwar and Chirand. The last site has yielded a corpus of bone tools and weapons including celts, scrapers, chisels, hammers, needles, points, borers, awls, arrowheads, etc. Other bone objects comprise ornaments like pendants, earrings, bangles, discs, combs, etc.

Terracotta objects including edge ground potsherds (triangular or rectangular in shape), spherical beads with central perforation were obtained from Senuwar. Chirand has yielded terracotta wheels, beads, bangles, cakes, birds, snakes, etc.

ORIGIN

The evidence of first farming and pastoral culture of the Vindhyas is the Neolithic culture. As revealed from the Mesolithic culture of the area, food processing equip-ments, wild animals and wild grains, which were domesticated/cultivated subsequently in the Neolithic period, microliths and bone tools, it can be inferred that the base for the Neolithic culture was being prepared in the Mesolithic period (Misra 2002). Neolithic culture of the Vindhyas is also credited with developing the Neolithic culture in the Gangetic plain as indicated by

comparative study of the culture of both the regions. The excavated sites of the Vindhyas and Ganga plain present ample evidence of cultural contact of both the regions. In the Western part of the mid Ganga valley, where preceding Mesolithic sites are in good number no Neolithic site was located earlier. The identification of Neolithic level at Jhusi and Hetapatti in Allahabad on the Ganga presents for the first time evidence of the Neolithic culture on the western margin of mid Ganga plain. There may be hidden some more Neolithic settlements in between the eastern and western margin of the area. The preceding Mesolthic culture of the Ganga valley contains food processing equipments made on sand stone/quartzite but no pottery, where as in the Vindhyas it is associated with hutments and hand made pottery also. Among the ceramic industries, the cord-impressed ware has much archaeological importance as it denotes the cultural contact of Vindhyas with that of the Ganga plain. The cord-impressed ware has been found in Neolithic context at Chirand, Chechar Kutub Pur, Taradih, Sohagaura, Lahuradeva, Jhusi and Hetapatti in the middle Gangetic plain that has techno-typological similarity with that of the Vindhyas. The evidence suggests that the Neolithic pottery of the middle Gangetic plainV has a considerable influence of the Vindhyan Neolithic pottery.[41] It is suggested that the Neolithic culture of the Gana plain owes to the Vindhyan Neolithic for its origin.

CHRONOLOGY

The problem of the antiquity of the Neolithic culture of the Vindhyas is still not finally settled but now we have some relevant C^{14} dates from the excavated Neolithic sites of the Vindhyas and Ganga plain. Considering three of C^{14} dates reading 4530±185 B.C. (PRL 101), 5440±240 B.C. (PRL 100) and 6570±210 B.C. (PRL 224) obtained from Koldihwa as dependable, the culture was dated to the 7th-6th millenium B.C. (Sharma *et al.* 1980). But doubts were raised about such early antiquity. The C^{14} date belonging to the transitional phase of the Neolithic to Chalcolithic is 1440±120 B.C. (PRL 223). The absolute dates obtained from Mahagara also indicated a late date to the culture, though these dates have the possibility of contamination of samples. Two TL dates 2265 B.C. and 1616 B.C. and four C^{14} dates 1440±150 B.C. (PRL 409), 1330±120 B.C. (PRL 408), 1440 ± 100 B.C. (PRL 407) and 1480 ± 110 B.C. (BSI) have been obtained from the samples from Mahagara. These dates are not consistent with the stratigraphy possibly due to contamination of samples. In the light of C^{14} dates obtained from Kunjhun, reading 4600±80 B.C., the revised chronology of the Vindhyan Neolithic culture was proposed to 4th millennium B.C. (Clark and Khanna 1989). Three C^{14} dates have come to light from recent excavations at Lahuradewa in the middle Gangetic plain which read as 5320±90 B.P. (BS 1951) (Cal B.C. 4220, 4196, 4161) and 6290±160 B.P. (BS 1966) (Cal B.C. 5298) (Tewari *et al.* 2001-2002, 2002-2003). Recently three relevant C^{14} dates have been obtained from Tokwa. When calibrated these read 6591 B.C. (BS − 2417), 5976 B.C. (BS − 2369), 4797 B.C. (BS − 2464). An AMS C^{14} date for a carbonized domesticated rice would push the antiquity of the Neolithic culture at Lahuradeva in 7th millennium B.C. (Tewari *et al.* 2005: 40). From the Neolithic horizon of Jhusi on the confluence of the Ganga-Yamuna in Allahabad three C^{14} dates have been obtained. These dates when calibrated, read 7477 B.C. (BS − 2526), 5837 B.C. (BS − 2524) and 6196 B.C. (BS − 2525). The earliest date obtained from the site would put the beginning of the Neolithic culture of the site in 8th millennium B.C.

The combined testimony of the available C^{14} dates obtained from Koldihwa, and Tokwa in the North-Central India and Jhusi and Lahuradeva in the middle Ganga plain would push the antiquity of the Neolithic culture in the northern Vindhyas and the middle Ganga plain to a hoary past. The antiquity of the early farming culture of the Gangetic plain on the basis of these dates may be pushed back to the later half of 8th millennium B.C. and almost same or slightly earlier antiquity may be proposed for the Neolithic culture of the Vindhyas.

References

ALLCHIN B. and F.R. ALLCHIN 1968. The Birth of Indian Civilization: India and Pakistan Before 5000 B.C.. Penguin Books, Harmondsworth.

ALUR, K.R. 1980. Faunal Remains from the Vindhyas and the Ganga Valley, in G.R. Sarma, V.D. Misra, D. mandal, B.B. Misra and J.N. Pal *et al* Beginnings of Agriculture, Abinash Prakashan, Allahabad.

CLARK, J. DESMOND and Gurucharan S. Khanna, 1989. The Site of Kunjhun II, Middle Son Valley, and its Relevance for the Neolithic of Central India, in J.M. Kenoyer (Ed.) Old Problems and New Perspectives in the Archaeology of South Asia. Wisconsin Archaeological Reports, Vol. 2, Department of Anthropology, University of Wisconsin, Madison: 29-46.

CHATURVEDI, S.N. 1985, Advances of Vindhyan Neolithic and Chalcolithic Cultures to the Himalayan Tarai: Excavations and Explorations in the Saryupar Region in Uttar Pradesh, Man and Environment, IX: 120 ff.

HARVEY, E.L., D. FULLER, J.N. PAL and M.C. GUPTA 2005. Early Agriculture of the Neolithic Vindhyas (North-Central India), South Asian Archaeology 2003, Ute Franke-Vogt and Hans-Joachim Weisshaar. (eds.). Linden Soft Verleg e. k. Aachen.

Le MESURIER, H.P. 1861. A Letter from H.P. Le Mesurier read during the proceedings of the Royal Asiatic Society of Bengal on January 14, 1861. Journal of the Royal Asiatic Society of Bengal 30 (1): 81-85.

MANDAL, D. 1997, Neolithic Cultures of the Vindhyas : Excavations at Mahagara in the Belan Valley in V.D.

Misra and J.N. Pal (Eds.) Indian Prehistory: 1980. Department of Ancient History, Culture and Archaeology, University of Allahabad.

MISRA, B.B. 2006. Koldihwa – A Key site for the Neolithic and Chalcolithic culture of the Vindhyas. Art, Archaeology and Cultural History India, (U.N. Roy Felicitation Volume, Part I), (Ed. C.P. Sinha).

MISRA, V.D. 1977. Some Aspects of Indian Archaeology. Prabhat Prakashan, Allahabad.

MISRA, V.D. 2002. Origin, Chronology and Transformation of the Mesolithic Culture in India, in Mesolithic India (V.D. Misra and J.N. Pal eds.), pp. 447-464. Department of Ancient History, Culture and Archaeology, University of Allahabad, Allahabad.

MISRA, V.D. n.d. Stone Age cultures, their Chronology and Beginning of Agriculture in North-central India, Presidential address presented in the Annual Conference of Indian Society of Prehistoric and Quaternary Studies, Jiwaji university, Gwalior, 2-5 december 2006.

MISRA, V.D., B.B. MISRA, J.N. PANDEY and J.N. PAL 1995-96, A preliminary report on the Excavations at Jhusi, 1995. Pragdhara No. 6, pp. 63-66.

MISRA, V.D., J.N. PAL and M.C. GUPTA 1998-89, Further Excavation at Jhusi, District Allahabad (Uttar Pradesh): 1998. Pragdhara No. 9, pp. 43-49.

MISRA V.D., J.N. PAL and M.C. GUPTA1999-2000, Further Excavations at Jhusi (1998-99), Pragdhara No. 10, pp. 23-30.

MISRA, V.D., J.N. PAL and M.C. GUPTA 2002-2003, Further Excavations at Jhusi: Evidence of Neolithic Culture, Pragdhara, No. 13. pp. 227-229.

MISRA, V.D., J.N. PAL and M.C. GUPTA, 2001, Neolithic Culture of the Northern Vindhyas with special reference to Tokwa, Bharti, Bulletin of the Department of Ancient Indian History, Culture and Archaeology, B.H.U. Varanasi 25 (I and II) 1998-99: 211-233.

MISRA, V.D., J.N. PAL and M.C. GUPTA, 2000-2001, Excavation at Tokwa: A Neolithic-Chalcolithic Settlement), Pragdhara, No. 11, pp. 59-72.

NARAIN, L.A. 1970, The Neolithic settlement at Chirand, The Journal of Bihar Research Society, 56: 16-35.

PAL. J.N. 1986, Archaeology of Southern Uttar Pradesh: Ceramic Industries of Northern Vindhyas, Swabha Prakashan, Allahabad.

PAL, J.N., 1987. Neolithic Cord-Impressed Ware of the Vindhyas, Man and Environment, XI, 61-65.

PAL, J.N. and M.C. GUPTA 2004. Significance of Recent Excavations at Tokwa in the Vindhya and Jhusi in the Gangetic Plain, Journal of Interdisciplinary Studies in History and Archaeology, Volume 1, Number 1 (Summer 2004), pp. 120-127.

PAL, J.N. and M.C. GUPTA 2005. Excavations at Hetapatti (Allahabad District): Some Preliminary

Observations Journal of Interdisciplinary Studies in History and Archaeology, Vol 2, No.1 (Summer 2005), pp. 163-168.

ROY, S.R. 1989, Chirand, A Encyclopaedia of Indian Archaeology, Vol. II (Ed. A. Ghosh), Munshiram Manohar Lal, New Delhi, pp. 103-105.

SHARMA, G.R., V.D. MISRA, D. MANDAL, B.B. MISRA, and J.N. PAL 1980. Beginnings of Agriculture, Abinash Prakashan, Allahabad.

SIGH, B.P. 1990, Early Farming Communities of Kaimur Foot Hills, Puratattva, 19: 6-18.

SINGH, B.P. 1997, Neolithic and Chalcolithic Pottery of Middle Ganga Plain: A Case Study of Senuwar, Ancient Ceramics (Historical Enquiries and Scientific Approaches) ed. P.C. Pant and Vidula Jayaswal, Agam Kala Prakashan, New Delhi.

SINGH, B.P. (Ed.) 2004, Early Farming Communities of the Kaimur (Excavations at Senuwar), Two volumes, Publication Scheme, Jaipur.

SINGH, P., 1992-93 Archaeological excavations at Imlidih-Khurd, Pragdhara No. 3, pp. 21-36; Singh, P. 1993-94, Further Excavations at Imlidih-Khurd, Pragdhara, No. 4, pp. 41-48; Singh, P., Ashok Kumar Singh and Indrajeet Singh, 1992, Excavations at Imlidih-Khurd, Puratattva, No. 22, pp. 120-22.

SINGH, P., and A.K. SINGH 1997-98, Trial Excavation at Bhunadih, District Ballia (U.P.), Pragdhara, No. 8, pp. 12-29.

SINGH, P., and A.K. SINGH 1995-96, Trial excavation at Waina, District Ballia (U.P.), Pragdhara, No. 6, pp. 41-61.

SINHA, H.P. 1994, Archaeological and Cultural History of Bihar, (with special reference to Neolithic Chirand), Ramanand Vidya Bhawan, New Delhi.

TEWARI, RAKESH, R.K. SRIVASTAVA and K.K. SINGH, 2002, Excavations at Lahuradeva, District Sant Kabirnagar, Puratattva, 32: 54-62.

TEWARI, RAKESH, R.K. SRIVASTAVA, K.K. SINGH, K.S. SARASWAT and I.B. SINGH, 2002-2003, Preliminary Report of the Excavations at Lahuradeva, District Sant Kabirnagar, U.P. 2001-2002: Wider Archaeological Implications, Pragdhara, 13: 37-68.

TEWARI, RAKESH, R.K. SRIVASTAVA, K.K. SINGH, RAM VINAY, RAJIV KUMAR TRIVEDI and G.C. SINGH 2004-2005, Recently Excavated Sites in the Ganga Plain and North Vindhyas: Some Observations Regarding the Pre-urban Context, Pragdhara, 15: 40-43.

VARMA, A.K. 1998, Neolithic Culture of Eastern India, Ramanand Vidya Bhawan, New Delhi.

VERMA, B.S. 1971, Excavations at Chirand: New Light on Indian Neolithic Complex, Puratattva, 4: 19-24.

VISHNU MITTRE and ARUNA SHARMA, n.d. Neolithic-Chalcolithic Food Economy of Eastern Uttar Pradesh.

AN EXPERIMENTAL STUDY ON THE MANUFACTURING PROCESS OF THE LOWER PALAEOLITHIC IMPLEMNETS FROM QUARTZ NODULES

Krishnendu POLLEY

Department of Anthropology, Calcutta University, 35, Ballygunge Circular Road, Kolkata 700 019
E-mail: krishnendu_polley@yahoo.com

Ranjana RAY

Professor Emeritus, Department of Anthropology, Calcutta University, 35, Ballygunge Circular Road, Kolkata 700 019.
Mailing address: 49/53, Prince Gulam Md. Shah Road, Kolkata 700 033. E-mail: prof.ranjana.ray@gmail.com

Abstract: Experiments with lithic technology helps Prehistorians to understand the nature and the evolution of technology manifested by the Stone Age people. Sometimes it also helps to understand the related behaviours like choice of raw materials as well as the biological abilities of prehistoric people. The latter directly or indirectly helped the process of evolution of culture. In India not much work is done on this aspect. Quartz is found to have been used in large quantity for manufacturing Lower Palaeolithic tool in Eastern part of India. This has been noticed both in the recent field work by the author in the Eastern Plateau region as well as in the collection made by the earlier Prehistorians from this region, which is stored in the prehistory museum of the department of Anthropology, Calcutta University. An experimental study on the manufacturing process of the Lower Plaeolithic implements from quartz nodules is carried out in order to shed more light on Lower Palaeolithic technology as well as related behaviours of the Lower Palaeolithic people.
Keywords: Palaeolithic, quartz, tools, technology, experiment, eastern India.

Résumé: L'experimentation en technologie lithique aide les Préhistoriens à comprendre la nature et l'évolution de la technologie manifesté par les hommes de l'Age de la Pierre. Parfois elle aide aussi a comrendre des comportements associés, tels que le choix des matières premières ou les compétences biologiques des peuples préhistoriques. Ces-ci on aidé, riecte ou indirectement, le processus d'evolution de la culture. En Inde il n'y a pas eu beaucoup de travail sur cet aspect. Le quartz a été utilisé en large quantité pour la manufacture d'outils au Paléolithique Inférieur, dans la partie orientale de l'Inde. Ceci fut noté soit dans les travaux de terrain récents de l'auteur dans le plateau oriental, soit dasn les collectins organisées par les premiers préhistoriens de la région, qui sont archivées dans le musée du département d'Anthropologie de l'Université de Calcuta. Une étude expérimentale du processus de manufacture des outils du Paléolithique Inférieur a partir de nodules de quartz a été poursuivi, pour mieux comprendre la technologie au Paléolithique inférieur ainsi que les comportements associés des hommes du Paléolithique Inferieur.
Mots-clés: Paléolithique, quartz, outils, téchnologie, expérimentation, Inde orientale

INTRODUCTION

Prehistoric Archaeology is almost entirely based on the study of the stone artefacts of prehistoric people. Lithic artefacts can be studied by three different ways, e.g., i) by studying the lithic artifacts themselves, ii) by experimental manufacture and use of similar artefacts and iii) by observing use or manufacture of similar artefacts among the people who may still be in a comparable cultural stage even today (Sankalia, 1964).

Out of these the second way of study and analysis of lithic artefacts, that is, by way of experimentation with lithic technology, is not a new branch in the field of prehistoric archaeology. In Europe it was started by Sven Nilsson in 1868 (Johnson, 1978) who for the first time experimenttally manufactured Palaeolithic tools from flint. Schleicher (1927) took up the work with the gun flint knappers of Europe. The tradition is still continuing with the brilliant works of Keeley (1980), Odell and Odell (1981), Crabtree (1982), Kobayashi (1985), Whittaker (1994), Debenath and Dibble (1994) and many other scholars. Unfortunately in India only a few experimental works on lithic technology are done so far. Sankalia has given a general account of the stone age tools, their techniques of manufacture, names and probable function

(Sankalia, 1964). In his book on the above he has mentioned about two archaeologists, Z.D. Ansari and P. R. Kulkarni, who were skilled in knapping stone tools and had experimentally made stone implements of different types and technique. Beside these works of Koshambi (1967), Shinde (1988) and Paddayya (2004) are of much importance in the Indian context.

A broad survey of the Palaeolithic cultures of India indicates that Palaeolithic people in this country used a large variety of raw materials for making their implements. Among these, quartzite and quartz were largely used. However, so far not much attention is paid on quartz as tool making raw material mostly because of the brittleness of the stone. In course of field work in the Tajna River valley, near Ranchi, the district head quarter of the state of Jharkhand, in Eastern India, both the authors found a large number of Lower and Middle Palaeolithic implements, which were mainly made on quartz nodules. More than 50% of the Palaeoliths from this area were made on quartz. This was an intriguing situation. Under the guidance of the second author the first author took up the work on experimenting with the manufacturing technique of stone tools on quartz. To make an in depth study of the manufacturing technique of the implements found at the sites, some replicas were made on quartz nodules selected from the Tajna river valley. Present paper describes the experiences with the experiment made by the authors with flaking of quartz nodules for manufacturing of stone tools similar to those of Lower and Middle Palaeolithic types that were found from the above mentioned sites.

METHODS

Preparatory stages

Stone hammers

In this experiment a total of eight hammer stones of different weights were selected for use. All of them were collected during the field work in the region selected as above. The following table shows weight and type of raw material of each of the hammers.

All the hammers selected were quartzite in nature. This was selected for its hardness and less brittle character. The weight of the hammers varied from 21.700 gm to 746.000 gm.

Bone hammer

In this experiment a small cylindrical shaped bone hammer (Museum no. C.M-2) was used for flaking stones. It was 5.5 cm long with a mean diameter of 1.5 cm and it weighed 10.9 gm.

Hammer No.	Weight (gm)	Raw Materials
1	162.900	Quartzite
2	164.400	"
3	70.000	"
4	43.500	"
5	26.700	"
6	21.700	"
7	31.700	"
8	746.00	"

Bone hammer needed a special method of preparation prior to its use. It may be mentioned here that the authors have prepared the hammer with the help of boiling and greasing but it might not have been the method followed by early man. No such hard piece of bone was found to be occurring in the locality and for the sake of present experiment the authors made the hammer in the laboratory in the method described below.

The hammer was made from a piece of the femur bone of a goat. It was actually the epiphyses of the femur, hollow along the marrow cavity. The piece of the bone was collected from a meat shop. The flesh present on its outer surface was scraped out with a sharp steel knife. After this the bone was boiled in water for thirty minutes. The remaining flesh on the outer surface of the bone and the marrow present in the cavity of the bone was removed by boiling. After the bone was boiled, it was left in shade for about six hours for the bone to dry in air. It was not exposed to direct sun. Drying under direct sun produces cracks on the bone. Finally the bone was smeared with grease. In this case the researcher used petroleum jelly. This gave the bone durability. It also moistened the surface of the hammer and prevented formation of cracks, which happen mainly due to dryness. Then one end of this bone was whittled with a knife. This pointed end may some times be used as a fabricator. The authors do not think that the early man produced his bone hammer in this way.

Raw Materials for Tool

The raw materials for this experiment were collected from the lower graved bed of Tajna river, from which the Lower Palaeolithic artefacts were found (Ghosh, 1977; Ray 1994). Rounded, slightly flattish and fresh quartz nodules, without any flaking on it were selected as raw materials for the present experimentation. Highly weathered nodules and those with weak lines were rejected.

Experimentation in the laboratory

Experiment was conducted in the laboratory of the department of anthropology, Calcutta University. The authors selected ten quartz nodules out of those collected from the field for manufacturing of stone implements. Only six implements could be successfully manufactured from the ten nodules selected. Out of these six artefacts, five were made on core and one was a flake tool. Description of method of flaking is given below.

The worker squatted down. The quartz nodule was held in his left hand. Then a direct blow with stone hammer was delivered on one edge of the nodule. At the time of striking, angle between the Hammer and the nodule, was approximately 120°. The worker held the hammer stone in this right hand. In this way a flake was removed from the under surface of the nodule, not from the surface on which the blow was given (fig. 6.1). The flake came out from the edge of the surface of the nodule on which the hammer was struck. Next blow was given at a point nearest to the flake scar taken out by previous flaking. The second blow was delivered in the same manner as the first. Another flake was detached and the scar was on the same surface as mentioned above. At the time of flaking it was noticed that if the second blow was given on the nearest surface of previous flake scar, then less amount of force was required compared to the force that was given in the first strike. If the second flake was detached somewhat away from the first flake scar, then more force was needed. When one surface was entirely flaked in this way, then the other surface was flaked in a similar manner. It may be pointed out that when the worker was

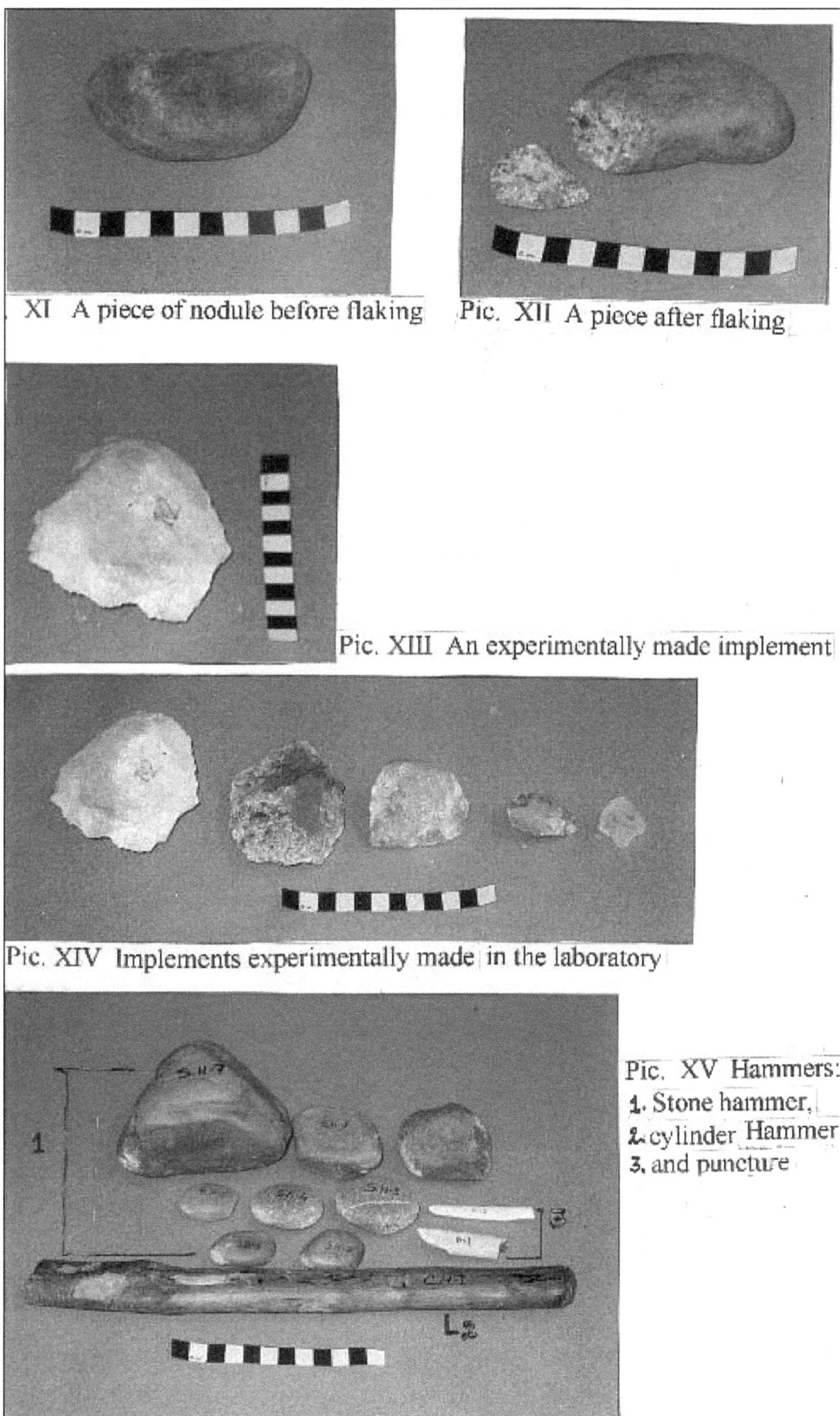

XI A piece of nodule before flaking

Pic. XII A piece after flaking

Pic. XIII An experimentally made implement

Pic. XIV Implements experimentally made in the laboratory

Pic. XV Hammers:
1. Stone hammer,
2. cylinder Hammer
3. and puncture

Fig. 6.1. Different stages of experiment on tool making

Tab. 6.1. Changes in the metric characters before and after flaking

specimen No.	metric features before & after flaking	weight (gm)	maximum length (cm.)	maximum Breadth (cm.)	maximum thickness (cm.)
I	Before	355.500	11.3	8.1	3.5
	After	217.000	9.4	6.8	3.1
II	Before	562.200	11.00	9.3	5.0
	After	271.000	11.20	8.7	4.6
III	Before	172.500	6.6	5.9	4.1
	After	135.500	6.1	5.5	3.9
IV	Before	64.00	5.3	3.7	2.2
	After	33.00	4.4	3.5	2.2
V	Before	76.900	4.9	5.0	2.1
	After	4.950	2.8	1.9	0.4
VI	Before	22.500	4.5	3.4	1.5
	After	10.400	4.1	2.7	1.1

working with the intention of flaking both surfaces of the nodule, he may detach flakes from both surfaces of the implement simultaneously or he may entirely work on one surface of the implement first and after that detach flakes from the reverse surface. In this way, the implements were primarily flaked in this experiment with the application of stone hammer technique in the laboratory.

Most of the implements prepared in the laboratory were with primary flaking. Only on two implements, (Mus. No. I-5 and Mus. No. I-6), retouching was done with the help of a cylindrical hammer. Retouching was done after an implement was primarily flaked and shaped. For this the implement was held in the left hand of the worker, a blow was delivered with the cylindrical hammer prepared for the purpose. Blow was given on one edge of the implement as per intention of the worker. In this way the secondary flakes were detached by the researcher. It is important that for secondary flaking the worker should deliver the blow straight on the edge of the implement. Because of the relative softness and rounded shape of the cylindrical bone hammer small and tiny flakes with flat bulbs of percussion were detached. Moreover, it made the edge of the implement sharper and straight.

OBSERVATION

Experiment conducted by the researchers has brought out a few interesting observations mainly on the raw materials used, wastages produced, size reduction of the material into final production, time required for the preparation of the implement, technique employed and finally on the finished product, that is, the tool type. Following tables show the major features of the experiment. Table 6.1 shows the metric characters before and after flaking of the materials into tools. Table 6.2 shows the amount of waste flake produced in gm. and percent of such waste in

relation to its original weight. The hammer types used for making of the implements are also presented in the table as well as the time involved.

CONCLUSION

Following conclusions are drawn from the total experimenttation, observation, and the results of production of all the six implements mentioned in this paper.

i. All the quartz nodules, which were selected for making implements are flattish in nature. Their maximum length and maximum breadth were greater than the maximum thickness. This observation and the personal experience of researcher put forward a fact that flattish nodules can be more easily flaked into an implement than the rounded nodules. Probably prehistoric man preferred to use flattish nodule for making of their implements.

ii. The second important observation is on the time required for manufacture of an implement. It cannot be simply explained that finely flaked implements took more time for their production. Time factor depends mostly on the hardness of raw material and to some extent on the method of flaking. Two examples may be sited here. Specimen-I was made by detaching a few flakes with the application of stone hammer. Flaking done in this method makes a 39% reduction in the weight of raw material, 16.80% reduction in length, 16.0 reduction in the thickness of raw material. It took 12 minutes for manufacturing of this implement. The raw material consisted of much hard quartz.

In case of specimen VI, simple stone hammer and cylinder hammer flaking together made about 54%

Tab. 6.2. Salient features of the experiment

Features		SPECIMENS					
		I	II	III	IV	V	VI
Waste Flake Produced	gm	138.500	291.200	37.00	31.00	71.950	12.100
	%	39	51.79	21.44	48.43	93.56	53.77
Reduction in Maximum length	cm	1.9	0.8	0.5	0.9	2.1	0.4
	%	16.8	7.27	7.57	16.98	42.85	8.88
Reduction in Maximum Breadth	cm	1.3	0.6	0.4	0.2	3.1	0.7
	%	16.04	6.45	6.77	5.40	62.00	20.58
Reduction in Maximum thickness	cm	0.4	0.4	0.2	0.0	1.7	0.4
	%	16.04	8.00	4.87	0.0	80.95	26.66
Time Required		12 mints.	5 mints. 20 sec.	4 mints.	6 mints.	4 mints.	8 mints.
Technique Applied & the hammers used		Stone hammer	Stone hammer	Stone hammer	Stone hammer	Stone hammer and Cylinder hammer	Stone hammer
Types of Implement produced		Hand Axe (On core)	Hand Axe (On core)	Chopper (On core)	Side Scraper (On core)	Side Scraper (On flake)	Point (On core)

reduction of the weight, 8.88% of the length, 20.58% breadth and about 26.66% of thickness of the original raw material. It took only 8 minutes for the production of the tool, which was finely flaked. The raw material in this case too is quartz, but possessed an unique isotropic character. The experiment reveals that the nature of raw material has a major impact upon the amount of time required to produce a tool. The tool makers of prehistoric time took cognizance of the character of the raw material as was found in an earlier research for the analysis of raw materials used by Palaeolithic tool makers of Eastern India. Thin sections of the tools were made and studied under microscope, which showed a definite selection of the raw materials by the makers (Ray *et al.,* 1997).

The method of flaking and the nature of tool has an important impact upon the time required for the production of an implement. Both the specimens V and VI are of same material, but the flake tool, which is made from specimen V took only 4 minutes 3 seconds for the completion of the tool, where as the core tool, made from specimen VI took about 8 minutes for the completion of the implement. It may be noted that in case of production of both core and flake tools different methods of flaking were used. Therefore it is clear that for production of an implement, the method of flaking and the finished implement type that was intended by the maker, have direct impact upon the amount of time taken

iii. The third important conclusion drawn is that secondary flaking done by cylinder hammer not only made the working edge of the implement straight, but it also reduced its breadth, as is observed in case of specimen VI.

iv. It may also be concluded that the type of experimentation conducted help us to understand how much debitage can be produced in the production of a particular kind of implement. Amount of debitage produced may be predicted from the type of implement found from the prehistoric sites. For example from specimen VI the most finely flaked core tool was made. It produced highest amount of debitage, where as the most coarsely flaked core implement made from specimen III, produced the lowest amount of waste flakes.

v. Finally present experimentation showed that a very small quantity of raw material is required for the production of a flake tool. A particular amount of raw material (e.g. 1000 gms) can produce only one core implement, but the same amount of raw material produced large number of flake implements.

vi. The personal experience of the first author at the time of flaking of the quartz implement indicated that flaking of quartz produced more dust than clearly defined flake. Clearly defined flakes in the present experiment are quite few in number.

vii. The present experimentation is a very small one. With more time and with more technical facility such work on experimental archaeology may throw light on the methods of study and interpretation of stone tools. If the number and nature of flakes produced from a particular raw material is recorded in each stage of manufacture, it can help in the understanding of two important aspects. Firstly, lithic reduction strategy of producing a particular type of implement, that is, core biface or flake tool may be understood (Nassony, 1996; Hayden *et al,* 1996). Secondly, proper cogni-

53

zance of lithic refitting study can be made. Lithic refitting study of a relatively undisturbed archaeological site may give important data regarding archaeological site disturbance process, modes of refuse accumulation and the occupational history of the site (Morrow, 1996). Experiment like the one undertaken here may give necessary data regarding the number and nature of flakes produced in each stage of manufacture of a tool. These data can farther be used for the identification of such stages and for the study of lithic refitting of a particular site.

References

DEBENATH, A and DIBBLE, H.L. 1994, Hand Book of Palaeolithic Typology (Vol.I): Lower and Middle Palacolithic of Europe. Philadelphia: University of Pennsyivania.

HAYDEN, B., FRANCO, N. and SPAFFORD, J. 1996, Evaluating lithic strategy and design criteria. In Stone tools: Theoretical insights into Human prehistory, (ed) George H. Odell. Plenum Press, NewYork and London.

JOHNSON, L.L. 1978, A History of Flint Knapping Experimentation (1836-1978), Current Anthropology. 19:337-72.

KEELEY, L. 1980, Experimental Determination of Stone Tool Uses. Chicago, University of Chicago Press.

KOBAYASHI, HIROAKI. 1985, The study of Accidental Breakage of Backed Blades. Lithic Technology. Vol-14, No-1, April, 1985; 16-26. The University of Texas at San Antonio.

KOSAMBI, D.D. 1967, Living Prehistory in India, Scientific American, 216(2): 104-14.

NASSONEY, M.S. 1996, The role of chipped stone in the political economy of social ranking. In Stone tools: Theoretical insights into Human prehistory, (ed) George H. Odell. Plenum Press, NewYork and London.

MORROW, T.M. 1996, Lithic refitting and archaeological site formation process: a case study from the Twin Ditch site, Greene county, Illinois. In Stone tools: Theoretical insights into Human prehistory, (ed) George H. Odell. Plenum Press, NewYork and London.

ODELL, G. and ODELL-VEERECKEN, F. 1981, Verifying the Reliability of Lithic Use Wear Assessment by "Blind Tests": the Low Power Approach, Journal of Field Archaeology, 7(1): 87-120.

PADDAYYA, K. 1983, The relevance of experimental approach in Indian prehistory. In Rangavalli: Recent Researches in Indology, Sri S. R. Rao Felicitation volume. (ed) A.V. Narasimha Murthi and B.K. Gururaja Rao. Sandeep Prakashan, New Delhi. pp 1-10.

PADDAYYA, K. 2004, Stone breaking and stone flaking. In Issues and themes in Anthropology: A Fetechrift in Honour of Prof. D.K. Bhattacharya. (ed) V.K. Srivastava and Manoj Kumar Singh. Palaka Prakashan, New Delhi. Pp. 71-82.

RAY, RANJANA, PRASAD, S. and BASU, U. 1997, Some stone tools from Jamara site, Malaygiri foothills, Orissa. Bulletin of the Indo-Pacific Prehistory Association, 3 (16): 33-34.

SANKALIA, H.D. 1964, Stone Age Tools: Their technique of Manufacture, Name and Use. Pune, Deccan College.

SCHLEICHER, C.H. 1927, Un industrie qui disparait: La taille des silex modernes, L'homme prehistoric, 14 (5-6): 113-133.

SHINDE, VASANT, 1988, An experimental study of the stone tool manufacturing, Bulletin of Deccan College post graduate and research Institute. 48-49:311-317.

WHITTAKER, J.C. 1994, Flint Kinapping: Making and Understanding Stone tools. University of Texas Press, Austin.

DOKRA CRAFT OF WEST BENGAL:
A LEGACY OF INDIAN ARCHAEOMETALLURGY

Falguni CHAKRABARTY

Department of Anthropology, Vidyasagar University, Medinipur, Pin 721102, India,
E-mail: falguni.mita@yahoo.co.in

Abstract: Metallurgy in Indian subcontinent dates back to circa 6000 B.C. with occurrence of a few copper objects, from the early phases of Mehergarh, Pakistan. However, in prehistoric times use of a more or less permanent mould to cast a number of articles, one after another, was unknown. One of the earliest methods of casting metal objects was to make a wax model of the article that was replaced by the molten metal, this being technically known as the lost wax or cire perdue process. The statue of the dancing girl, unearthed at Mohenjodaro dated around third millennium B.C. with intricate but elegant carving, shows that the cire perdue process had already been perfected.

This process has presently been highly marginalized globally by the process of industrialization. The various tribal communities, however, living in different regions of India even today continue to practice this prehistoric craft for living. These craftsmen and their craft are respectively known by different names in different regions of India. One such community living in West Bengal, a state in India, is known as Dhokra and the craft they follow is regionally known by the same name of their community.

With this background, the present paper aims to highlight the variations of technology, raw materials and types of produced items found among the Dhokra communities living in different districts of West Bengal. The paper, primarily based on ethno-archaeological approach, could be helpful to get some ideas about socio-cultural backdrop necessary for the continuity of a particular prehistoric trait on the one hand and the variation of the same trait in the context of time and space on the other.

Keywords: Archaeometallurgy, Dhokra, West Bengal, lost wax, ethno-archaeology

Résumé: La métalurgie dans le sub-continent Indien date de c. 6000 BC, avec l'occurrence de quelques objets en cuivre, des phases initiales de Mehergarth, au Pakistan. Pourtant, l'usage de moules plus ou moins permanents pour la production de plusieurs objets, l'un après l'autre, n'était pas connu en Préhistoire. Une des méthodes plus anciennes de production d'objects de metal était de faire un modèle en cire, lequel était remplacé par le métal fondu, ceci étant connu comme la méthode de la cire perdue. La statue de la fille dançante, fouillée à Mohenjodaro, datée autour du III milénaire BC, avec des garvures intriquées mais élégantes, montre que le processus de cire perdue était déjà parfait.

Ce processus a été largement marginalisé globalement, par le processu d'industrialisation. Les différentes comunautés tribales, pourtant, vivant en de différentes régions de l'Inde, continue a practiquer cet art pour survivre. Cest artisans et leur arts sont connus par de différents noms dans les différentes régions de l'Inde. Une communauté qui vie au Bengal ocidental, un État de l'Inde, est connu comme Dhokra, et l'art qu'elle poursuit est régionalement connue par le mêmem nom d ela cummunauté.

Avec ce contexte, l'article a pour but de éclaircir les variations de technologie, matières premières et types d'objects produits qui se trouvent chez les Dhokra vivant au Bengal occidental. L'article, basée en premier sur une approche ethno-archéologique, peut être utile à obtenir des idées sur le contexte socio-culturel nécéssaire à la continuité d'un trait préhistorique particulier, dans côté, et la variation de ce trait même dans le contexte du temps et de l'espace, de l'autre.

Mots-clés: Archéométalurgie, Dhokra, Bangal occidental, cire.perdue, ethno-archéologie

INTRODUCTION

The beginning of metallurgy in Indian subcontinent may be traced back to circa 6000 B.C with the occurrence of a few copper objects, from the early phases of Mehergarh, Pakistan. Probably copper was the earliest non-ferrous metal which man shaped in to tools for its lightness and resistance to corrosion. Later bronze, an alloy prepared from the metals namely copper, tin and zinc, was used for manufacture of metal objects.

However, in prehistoric times use of a more or less permanent mould to cast a number of articles, one after another, was unknown. One of the earliest methods of casting metal objects was to make a wax model of the article that was replaced by the molten metal, this being technically known as the lost wax or *cire perdue* process. The statue of the dancing girl, unearthed at Mohenjodaro dated around third millennium B.C. with intricate but elegant carving, shows that the *cire perdue or* lost-wax

process had already been perfected. From the limited domestic field, this metal ware gradually spread out in different directions, especially into the prestigious ritualistic field. In fact, the range in metal ware seems unlimited (Chattopadhyay 1975).

The legacy of archaeometallurgy, particularly hollow casting of metal by lost-wax process, is being carried on in India by a number of indigenous ethnic communities from the immemorial period of time. The ethnological details of the prehistoric techniques of metallurgy followed till today by these communities may help us to reconstruct different aspects of archaeometallurgy of the men of prehistoric and protohistoric period. The importance of such ethnological evidences became the matter of consideration among the researchers on archaeometallurgy in India in the recent time (Tripathi 1998). The products of process that went on in the past can be interpreted in terms of the process that can be observed at work at the present time (Trigger 1970).

In one of the main areas of Neolithic sites in West Bengal, a state of India, we find a small indigenous community engaged in the work of manufacturing metal wares by lost-wax process. These hollow-casting artisans are locally known as *Dokra* and some time considered as one of the division of Hindu caste *kamar or* blacksmith (Risley 1891). Similar artisan groups living in West Bengal are known as *Sekra, Mal, Thetri, and Malar etc.* A section of these artisan communities has adopted both Hindu and Muslim religion. (Census of India 1961) Their crafts and products are popularly known by the name of their community.

The products of the Dokra artisans are primarily made of brass (an alloy of copper and zinc) and bell-metal (a mixture of copper and tin). However, some of them also use alloy of aluminum particularly to cater the poor rural customers. The metal wares by the *Dokras* may be roughly divided into religious images, ritualistic items, objects of utility, ornaments, and decorative items.

THE METHODS AND MATERIALS

For the collection of data on various technological aspects of the *Dokras* the present author followed various standard anthropological methods of ethnographic field investigations. These methods may be broadly subdivided in to secondary sources and primary sources. Under the secondary sources, documents like Government publications, earlier research reports and Census reports are considered. Under the primary sources, participation observation and interview with the help of structured and unstructured questionnaires, genealogical methods have been followed.

The Dokras are living primarily in the rural areas of the districts of Bankura, West Midnapur, Purulia, Birbhum, and Burdwan all located in the Western part of West Bengal, India. Among these five districts except Burdwan, which is contiguous to Birbhum, remaining four districts form one of the main areas of Neolithic cultures of West Bengal and they are all part of the Chhotanagpur plateau (Sankalia 1974). These places are about 150 to 250 Km away from the city of Kolkata. The Dokras usually form a kind of small satellite settlement of temporary nature around the tribal and peasant villages in the rural parts of West Bengal. Therefore, owing to the shifting nature of the Dokras, the present author could not traverse all of their small settlements. So the Dokras of Bankura, Midnapur and Burdwan who are leading a sedentary life for at least last four decades, are considered for the present paper. The distribution and population of these Dokra settlements is given in Table 7.1.

Despite the migratory character of the Dokra community, the above table shows a relatively larger settlement at Bikna and Dariapur. This is due to the fact that Government of West Bengal has provided small houses along with common courtyard free of cost in these two

Tab. 7.1. Distribution and population of Dokhra settlements

District	Settlements	No. of Household	Total population
Bankura	Bikna	31	176
	Patrasayer	01	06
Burdwan	Dariapur	19	117
West Midnapur	Salgeria	03	12
GRAND TOTAL		54	311

localities for the permanent settlements of the Dokra community. Of all the settlements of Dokra artisans of West Bengal, those at Dariapur and Bikna have been organized as Industrial cooperatives by the ends of 1962 and 1965 respectively. The artisans of these two settlements have come in to contact with the organized market at the initiative of the State Government.

TECHNIQUES OF LOST-WAX PROCESS FOLLOWED BY THE DOKRAS

For metal casting by "lost-wax process" the Dokra artisans of West Bengal generally use the metal consisting of scrap of broken discarded bell-metal pots and pans, which are sold at a cheap rate in the local market. This does not mean that the artisans are careless about the metal they use. Actually, they choose and classify the scrap with discriminating care and blend them suitably. In case of raising the proportion of copper they occasionally use fresh sheet-brass cuttings along with brass scraps when necessary. The proper proportion is 60:40 between copper and zinc. However, the artisans who are recently being trained and financially promoted by the Government agencies try to use virgin brass-metal sheets as much as possible. However, to cater the need of the poor tribal communities the Dokras of West Bengal also use the scrap of aluminum objects.

The details of the techniques of manufacture followed by the Dokras of West Bengal have been reported by various authors from time to time. Some of these authors were Government officials where as some others were professional sculptors. The names of such authors, which deserve special mention, are A.N. Mukherjee (1961) and M. Mukherji (1977). Their descriptions are so fascinating that the present author cannot help echoing some of their valuable findings in his present paper.

The details of the different stages of techniques of lost-wax process of brass-metal casting followed by the Dokra artisans of West Bengal may be subdivided under different broad subheadings and they are namely: predesigning stage; designing and covering up stage; precasting and preparatory stage; casting stage; post-casting and finishing stage. The descriptions of these stages are given in the following paragraphs:

Predesigning Stage

Core buildings

For making the Core, the craftsman procures plastic clay from the fields around the village and the ponds. He collects paddy-husk pounded into finer bits. Clay is mixed with water and paddy-husk and kneaded to the consistency of modeling clay. The clay and paddy-husk are in the proportion of about 2:1. This mixture is so soft that only the simplest suggestions of a form can be achieved, laying it flat on a clear floor. It is possible that the soil they use is already sufficiently cracked resisting. This first skeleton of the core is then covered with a layer of loose, fine and sandy clay. Subsequently, dry core is scraped with bits of broken earthenware. The scrapings are collected and mixed with water and the resulting paste is smeared over the core to serve as a polish.

Each core is a different one and a piece of creative art. The form of the object, subject to its specifications for height, is manifested gradually in the work with the fingers. Generally, for the hands and legs of a small object, plastic clay is used which is not needed to be removed after casting. But for the body of a bigger one although same variety of clay is used but the same is needed to be removed. The core is intended to represent the inner support of the design of the figure in green stage and is the hollow space inside the cast object. For measurements, no scale is used. The work of fingers is always accurate without any aid.

For the perfection and proper balance of the clay modeling work, the artisan keeps in view the ultimate metallic figure, which is retained when there is no longer, any core. For a smaller object, it is a single core, for a larger one; there are parts, which are attached to one another after being dried (or, for still bigger and complicated items, after casting, by soldering). The sun-dried core is slightly wetted and the artisan then smoothens its surface with fire clay and gives proper shapes by pinching and pressing in critical points.

Wax Preparation

When the plastic clay and strained clay are ready wax is prepared from resin, the source of which is Sal tree (*Shorea robusta*). The resins are purchased from the local markets by the artisans. Lump of resin is first broken into small pieces by a hammer and put on an open earthen vessel in finer particles by a scrapper. The vessel is heated on an oven with brick/stone supports and firewood. As soon as resins melts, mustard oil is added and allowed to form a liquid black compound. Resins and mustard oil are required in 5:2 proportions. The liquid is then poured into a vessel of cold water through a still mild hot and is converted by hand into thick sticks. This is used as wax.

Designing and Covering up stage

Wax-design around the Core

Resin-wax sticks are then heated in required quantities on mild fire of wood/ charcoal, which burn when the artisans busy in design work. The quantity of wax as well as the quantity of brass-metal necessary for any object is determined by its size. After all, it is the space to be released by the wax replica that is filled in by the molten metal. The proportion of brass metal to resin is generally 12:1 (by weight). Heating and lengthening of elastic wax sticks to desired thickness and diameter for tapes and wires are done concurrently. The artisan imagines the thickness of the metal product in different proportions and draws the thickness of wax accordingly. The threads are joined together to make strips of one-fourth to half width. Then it is a process of careful wrapping of the core with the strips followed up by decorative work with finer threads, here and there, as necessary requiring thread pieces of different thickness and lengths to be dove-tailed or wrapped in the continuing process. He uses a small iron flat piece to press, give cut marks or to cut off the thread. The final form is always the metallic form that emerges after the wax designs of given thickness and continuity wither away. The form now corresponds to the specific vision in the artisan's eyes with the accurate sense of spacing, balance and art of the artisan while reproducing a figure. The skin of wax coating gets gradually a living character when the parts of the figures are added and the ornaments of different motifs are set with the manipulation of wax threads.

Channel building

Subsequently, on the finished wax figure, the artisan provides an opening or channel in the highest point of the model to make freeway for the molten metal. The channels are wax rods sufficiently thick to make for easy flow of the metal. The obvious intention is to provide for an inlet for the molten metal to flow in the vacuum of lost wax most conveniently. Incidentally, the artisans now a day sometimes settle for tar in lieu of wax or resins in consideration of the expenditure involved.

Covering the wax

The artisan then covers the wax-model, except the tips of the wax channel, first with strained clay, and then with plastic clay and sand. Thus the waxwork remains round the hardcore and inside the outer clay mould. The finer clay cover catches up the design of the model in its exact shape, size and motif. The thickness of the surface clay is generally half-inch, sufficient to stand firing and to retain molten metal without damage.

Precasting and Preparatory Stage

Crucible building

The artisan then builds up the crucible to act as the container of the scrap brass-metal pieces to retain them

Tab. 7.2. Relationship between height and weight of a product in its final form

Category according To height	Raw metal required before casting	Weight of item in final form
(i) Within 3 inches	250 gramme	100-200 gramme
(ii) Within 6 inches	500 gramme	Within 400 gramme
(iii) Within 12 inches	1.5-2.5 kilograms	1-2 kilogram

until the molten metal flows in to the vacuum. It is made of plastic clay and its hollow space is determined on assumption of the quantity of metals to be put in. It is fixed on the already-made mould around the wax-runner with clay-paste being then added on the sides of the two items (mould and crucible) to turn them into one mould. The whole thing is dried in the open.

Crucible channeling

Two clay pipes form the path from the wax-model to the crucible. The feet of the pipes enclose the tips of the wax channel, and the heads join to form a single funnel. Then two sticks of bamboo are sent down through the pipes so that there is a straight free passage from the funnel mouth to the wax tips. When this attachment is dry, the bamboo sticks are withdrawn.

Crucible fitting

Then the brass-scraps are heated in fire of dung cake and coal for being broken in pieces with strokes of a hammer. For large objects, fresh brass-sheets are also mixed. The quantity needed for casting is determined on the basis of the size of the metal object along with its detailed and minute physiological and decorative parts. The metal required for the casting is worked out on the basis of a proportion of 10 metal to 1 wax. The wax used in the model is weighed before use. These small bits of metal are put inside the crucible. A crucible has generally a capacity to contain metal weighing up to one kilogram to two kilogram.

The artisan then covers up its mouth with mud and sand leaving a small opening with a piece of torn cloth on it at a point which is the top of the mould.

It is also to be mentioned here that, for some of the bigger items of composite nature separate castings are made, two or three in number, as necessary, which are joined together by soldering later on. The following Table 7.2. will show the relationship between the height of a usual product and its weight in final form as well as the quantity of metal initially required:

Furnace

The artisan mostly uses the yard in front of his house for a furnace. Furnace is built above the ground. Facing the direction of the wind, the frontage of the furnace is set on the opening ground with a few bricks and mud clusters forming a semi-circular wall of about 10" to 15" height. They rely on the natural draft. For this purpose they place gaps between the bricks. They reinforce the natural draft by indigenous winnowing fans. Inside are kept firewood, steam coal and cow-dung cakes. The fuel is charged from the walls to the center.

Casting stage

A layer of wood charcoal covers the bottom of the furnace upon which the figure is kept upright, with the crucible below it. It is held in position by logs piled on top of one another in triangular formation around and over the figure. The bottom logs are dry wood and serve for kindling, while the upper logs are green and serve to reduce overheating which causes cracks in the clay. These are again covered with fuel on all sides. The heating takes from two and a half to three hours, during which time the fire is slowly and steadily fanned with a bamboo-basket made winnowing fan.

Generally, a furnace accommodates the articles of one type. At a lower end of fuel, fire starts with burning of kerosene oil and, in two hours' time, the temperature attains about 1100°C. Before that point of heat, the wax melts and is converted into gas and is released through the crucible opening. The metal pieces melt around peak heat point. The full melting is ensured by the articles by visual inspection of the colour of flame (greenish-yellowish) and poking a stick inside to stir the material properly. It takes place when, the internal heat is sufficient and has been adequately available to the articles. He then brings out the mould with a pair of tong and with the help of an assisting hand, gets the leaking portions of wax-core quickly repaired by mud-plasters to avoid any wastage by oozing out of molten metal. The artisan shakes the mould gently and invert it so that the crucible is on top and the figure directly below it. The molten metal then flows from the crucible along the clay pipe and runner channels into the mould. The wax has in the mean time burnt out, leaving a free channel throughout the figure for the metal to flow through. After the pouring, the moulds are kept aside.

Post-casting and finishing stage

After the object is cooled by sprinkling of water the artisan uses either a chisel or an iron rod to break the clay forming outer mould and to remove the inner core. As there is plastic clay by and large, the composition of clay loosens after firing and it become easier to take out the inner core. Still the artisan has to be very cautious in giving stroke and in scrubbing, to avoid any damage of the cast metal. Previously, in general, for smaller pieces, the artisan did not remove the fired clay from inside the cast object. But after training by different Government agencies the artisan tries to remove such clay from all medium and big-size objects excepting the very small ones.

After the figure is recovered from the mould and the runner channels cutout, finishing begins. The different portions of the body are cleansed with a hard wire brush with the intention to remove the small clay particles deposited here and there and not to disturb the surface roughness as such, which is regarded as an integral aspect of the *Dokra* art. Soft soldering repairs the minor damages on the cast metal body and the excess deposits of metal inside the form are chiseled out. In any case, there is no general filing of the surface.

Despite craftsmanship there occasionally occur some defective productions. These defects occur when the appropriate shape and delicate decorations are not manifested properly. The damages are often due to the use of bad quality of brass metal resulting in relative hardness of cast form. These damages are due to the absence of the required malleability of the raw metal. The artisans purchase brass scraps, the quality of which has been rapidly deteriorating for the overall shortage of virgin non-ferrous items of copper and zinc and rising prices of used utensils. There is more of zinc than copper, thus disturbing the 60:40 (copper: zinc) ratio. Defects also occur when the resin fixing has no minimum thickness resulting in holes on cast body or when there is air blocking inside or when the metal is poured in before natural melting.

THE TOOLS AND EQUIPMENTS OF THE *DOKRA* ARTISANS

i. Earthen vessels for preparing liquid resin wax and cooling it.

ii. Crucible for melting brass-metal scraps.

iii. A small iron flat piece for cutting wax-threads when required and drawing the designs on the wax model. It is three inches to eight inches long.

iv. Anvil, hammer and chopper for breaking and cutting the brass metal into pieces and to break open the fired mould after casting.

v. Tongs, small (one foot) and big (two to three feet) size for holding the hot metal pieces to break in to small sizes; and for lifting the hot mould from furnace.

vi. Chisel, iron wire brush (five to six inches long), file, 12 inches hacksaw, table-vice, hand Drill (1/6", 1/8"), pliers (flat and round mouth, 6"), blowlamp and

blower are all recent additions at the instance of the Government agencies.

DIVISION OF LABOR AMONG THE *DOKRA* ARTISANS

The women participate in the following areas

Collection of basic clay; puging (and kneading) the clay with husk; preparation of coating clay cleansing dust and other particles by levigation and straining; assisting the male artisan in all other processes of clay work, firing, filing and cleansing etc.

The men folk are particularly engaged in the following activities areas

Procurement of metal; preparation of mould; wax modeling; filling in of crucible with metal pieces; firing and casting; marketing.

The Children of the Dokra artisans' family are partners in the production process and the maintenance of a technique tradition. The children participate from an age of 8-10.

THE PRODUCTS OF THE DOKRAS

Traditionally, the *Dokras* artisans produce such items, which have the demand among the rural tribal and peasant customers living around them. These products are primarily religious items, objects of domestic utility and ornaments for women folk. These products are usually of small sizes up to three inches to six inches height except the ladle, which are twelve to fourteen inches in length. The lists of such items are given in the Table 7.3.

The time-honored craft of the *Dokras* was faced with the possibility of extinction as in the changing industrial and urban scenario a section of poor artisans was forced to abandon their craft in favor of other jobs like soldering or working under rural goldsmith where their native skill could be more profitably used.

Things, however, began to change with the government stepping in with the objectives of promoting this indigenous craft and providing relief to the poor artisans. The artisans are now being trained to produce new items with news design as well as bigger size to meet the recent demands of the urban customers. It is observed that dominance of religious items earlier produced by the *Dokra* artisans are gradually being replaced by the decorative items and the objects of utility as per the demand of the urban customers. There is now, as a result, freer use of virgin metal in lieu of scrap metals.

The list of the items produce the dokras for the urban customers has been furnished in the Table 7.4.

Tab. 7.3. List of religious items

Religious items	Objects of utility
Hindu mythological figures like *Lakshmi* on elephant; *Jagannath*; *Narayan; Ganesh; Siva; Ganga; Dhanakuber; Bhagabari; Krishna; Radha; Saraswati; Durga; Viswakarma; Sabitri-Satyaban, Jagadhatri;* Owl; Incense burner; Lamp; Cluster of five lamps; Bell for worship etc.	Grain measuring bowls of five pieces; anklet for livestock, cattle bell, collyrium container, ladle, anklet for women, foot bangle, vermillion container etc.

Tab. 7.4. Items produced for urban customers

Religious images	Objects of utility	Decorative items and ornaments
Hindu mythological figures on cart or boat; *Kali, Snake-Pyramid, Ravana,* etc.	Door handle, brackets, candle stand, pen stand, ash-tray, coin box, paper weight, owl shaped container, water vessel, round tray, round powder box, small oval tray, rose bowl on three legs, tumbler (both big and small) etc.	Flower vase, wall hanging, figures of birds, fish, deer, peacock, horse, tortoise, frog, camel, elephant drawn chariot, bullock cart with passenger, images from popular rhyme, necklace, bangle, pendants, ear-rings etc. figures representing variety of rural activities etc.

CONCLUSION

The main contention of the present paper therefore, is that the techno-economic aspects of the *Dokra* craft of West Bengal desperately needs a well-orchestrated effort on the part of ethnographers in collaboration with other disciplines like metallurgy, archaeology etc. to make further documentation in a more comprehensive way. It is essential for the pristine forms of this prehistoric craft to remain recorded in a minute detail because they are constantly under threat of being either changed or destroyed by the pressure of modern times. The better we can record the pristine form, the easier will it be for the researchers to reconstruct different aspects of archaeometallurgy in India. The spatial variations of various attributes of archaeometallurgy in India can also be appreciated and may be reconstructed if the lost-wax process of metal casting followed by the Dokras of West Bengal is studied in relation to similar craft traditions still surviving among other indigenous communities in different parts of India like Orissa, Bihar, Madhya Pradesh, Maharastra etc. Here is a precious legacy of prehistoric tradition of technology and art that posterity should not willingly let dies.

References

CHATTOPADHYAY, K. 1975. *Handicrafts of India.* New Delhi: Wiley Eastern Limited.

MUKHERJEE, A.N. 1961. Dokra Artisans of Dariapur in *Census of India* 1961, West Bengal & Sikkim, Volume XVI, Part VII-A (4).

MUKHARJI, M. 1977. *Folk Metal Craft of Eastern India.* New Delhi: All India handicrafts Board.

PELTO, PERTTI J. and G.H. PELTO. 1978. *Anthropological Research: The structure of inquiry.* Cambridge University Press. Cambridge.

RISLEY, H.H. 1891. *Tribes and Castes of Bengal.* Calcutta. Bengal Secretariat Press. Reprinted and Published in 1998 by P. Mukharjee, Calcutta.

SANKALIA, H.D. 1974. *The Prehistory and Protohistory of India and Pakistan.* Poona, India: Deccan College Postgraduate and Research Institute.

TRIGGER, B.G. 1970. Aims in Prehistoric Archaeology. *Antiquity* 44:26 – 37.

TRIPATHI, V. 1998. "Iron Working in Ancient India – A Case Study" In Archaeometallurgy in India. Edited by Vibha Tripathi, PP: 209 – 217. New Delhi: Sharada Publishing House.

TRIPATHI, V. (Ed) 1998. *Archaeometallurgy in India,* New Delhi: Sharada Publishing House.

STUDIES ON A HUMAN BABY FOSSIL ENTOMBED WITHIN THE FERRICRETE

P. RAJENDRAN

UGC Research Scientist-C, Archaeologist, Dept.of History, Kerala University, Kariavattom-695581, Kerala, India.
E-mail:drprajendran@yahoo.co.in

Abstract: A suspected faunal fossil was discovered on 14th Oct. 2001 within the ferricrete at Odai in Bommayarpalayam in Villupuram district of Tamil Nadu in South India. In order to prove the existence of a faunal fossil within the ferricrete it was subjected to various medical methodology such as X-ray (CT), 2 D scan, 3 D scan, Photo Microscopy(3D), and Scanning Electron Microscopy. X-ray had identified, for the first time, the presence of a faunal fossil within the ferricrete. Subsequently 2 D scanning was applied and could distinguish the human cranium within the ferricrete. Then with the 3 D scanning hundreds of images were taken and they had proved it as a human baby skull. Photo Microscopy had identified 3 cervical vertebrae with the skull. It was further studied under SEM to understand various characteristics in detail and had well recorded fossilized cranial bone structure, blood vessels, membranous tissues, brain, RBC in dumbbell shape etc. In this contest the absence of any micro organisms within the skull is significant. In order to make one to one comparison a human foetus skull was examined under SEM. These studies proved beyond doubt that the entombed fossil belonged to a human baby.

The perfect nature of the fossilized RBC, brain tissues, membranous tissues, blood vessels and bone structure etc in fact shows unique kind of preservation of the fossil within the ferricrete. This might be due to the peculiar nature of the cyst formation over the fossil and also due to the absence of any micro organisms within the fossil. It has proved, for the first time, that the organic matter within the sediment was retained in fossil form even after the ferricretization of the matrix. Integrated multidisciplinary studies are in progress to unravel hither to unknown factors responsible for such a fossilization and preservation of the organic remains within the ferricrete.

Keywords: Ferricrete, baby, cranium, SEM, photomicroscopy

Résumé: Un fossile de faune a été découvert le 14 Octobre 2001, dans la crête ferrugineuse d'Odai à Bommayarpalayam, dans le département de Villupuram de Tamil Nadu, dans l'Inde du Sud. Pour prouver l'existence de faune dans la crête ferrugineuse il fut soumis à plusieurs méthodes médicales telles que le rayon-X (CT), scan 2D, scan 3D, photo microscopique (3d) et microscope élétronique a balayage. Le rayon X a identifié, pour la première fois, la présence de fossiles de faune dans la crête. Alors, avec le 3D des centaines d'images furent prises et elles ont prouvé la présence d'un crâne humain de bébé. La photo microscopique a identifié 3 vertèbres cervicales avec le crâne. Il fut alors étudié avec le SEM pour comprendre plusieurs caractéristiques en détail, et a bien enregistré une structure osseuse craniale fossilisée, des vases de sang, des restes de membranes, du cerveau, RCB etc. Dans ce contexte, l'absence de micro-organismes dans le crâne est significative. Pour faire une comparaiseon un à un, un crâne de phoetus fut examiné avec le SEM. Ces études ont prouvé au delà des doutes que le fossile trouvé était d'un bébé humain.

La nature parfaite du RBC fossilisé, des éléments de cerveau, des vases de sang et de la structure osseuse, etc., en faite démontre le type unique de préservation du fossile dans la crête. Ceci peut être du à la nature péculiaire de la formation de ciste sur le fossile, aussi due à l'absence de micro-organismes dans le fossile. Il a prouvé, pour la première fois, que la matière organique dans le sédiment fut conservée sous forme fossile même après le ferruginoisement de la matrice, Des études multidisciplinaires intégrées sont en cours pour comprendre les facteurs méconnus responsables pour cette fossilisation et préservation de restes organiques dans la crête.

Mots-clés: Ferrugineuse, bébé, crane, SEM, photomicroscope

INTRODUCTION

Large number of hominid fossils, rang from a few lacks to over three million year old, are known from different parts of World and many of them are found in stratified context. However, none of them was seen within the hard ferricrete and therefore, they could be retrieved out of the matrix. This is for the first time a human fossil has been discovered within the ferricrete of the Middle Pleistocene (Fig. 8.1a).

The entombed nature of the suspected fossil left no chance for excavation. In such a context the normal procedure is to extract the fossil in its entirety from the matrix either chemically, by dissolving the matrix away to leave the fossil or by dissolving the fossil away to leave a hole, or physically by digging the fossil out of the matrix. In this case, none of these approaches was particularly useful, and therefore, it was dug out along with the surrounding ferricrete. The entombed nature of the fossil makes visual examination impossible (Fig. 8.1b) and, therefore, strenuous effort was made to find out some other alternative for it's examination and identification.

METHODOLOGY

During the probe it was decided to take-up various Radiological methodology which are being used exclusively for medical purpose.

Initial attempts were made with X-ray Computed Tomography (CT) in which X-rays were passed into the specimen from 360 and detected by a row of detectors in opposite side. The difference in the density of the material is reflected as the intensity of X-rays. This difference is

Fig. 8.1a. Panoramic view of the Hominid site at Odai

Fig. 8.1b. Human fossil within the ferricrete

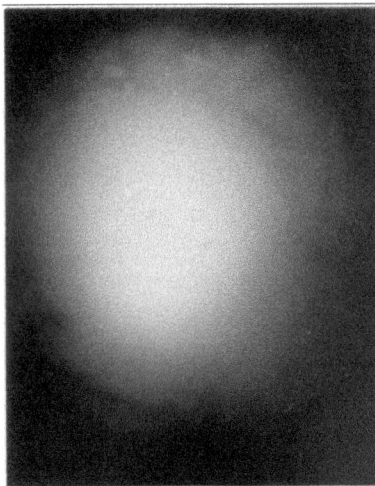

Fig. 8.1c. X-ray (CT) Image of
the Human fossil

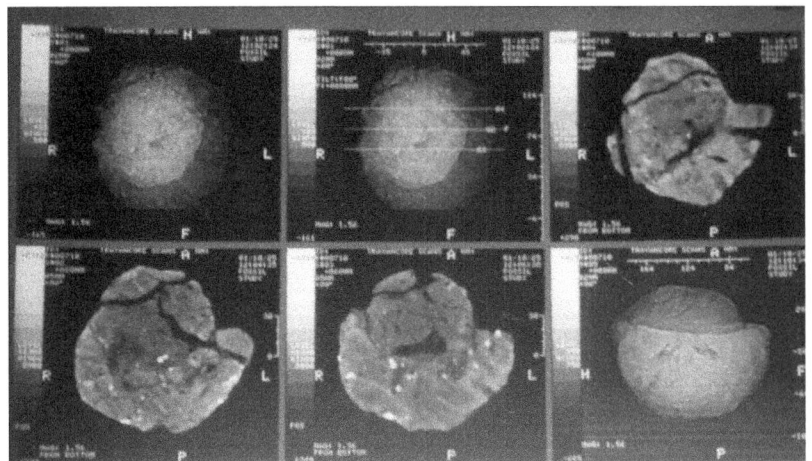

Fig. 8.1d. Cranial identification through 2D scanning

projected as an image by a complicated reconstruction algoritham. Thus an oval structure surrounded by the hard matrix has been identified and has confirmed, for the first time, the existence of a faunal fossil within the ferricrete (Fig. 8.1c). This stands contrary to the general belief among the geologists that on ferricretization of a fluvial deposit any organic material embedded in it gets destroyed or disappear. But this has established the fact that even after ferricretization of the alluvial matrix the faunal material did exist within it in fossil form.

Application of 2 D scanning has been attempted further to unravel various characteristics of the entombed fossil. Under it AP Scanogram slice from above, AP Scanogram with image planes, Cross-sectional images, and lateral Scanogram viewed from the side were carried out (Fig. 8.1d). These images have proved it as a human cranium.

The next step, based on the 3 D morphology reconstruction of the Herefordshire fossil (Briggs and Crowther. 2001), was carried out in order to extract all the cranial signatures of the fossil. Under it the scanning in thin helical runs (3 mm x 4.5 mm) of the entire specimen on

different planes were taken and reconstructed hundreds of images at 2 mm interval (Fig. 8.2a). They have revealed various signatures of a human baby skull (Fig. 8.2b) and have identified fossilized eye within the eye orbits (Fig. 8.2c), teeth within the mandible and maxilla, brain tissues and skull bones etc (Rajendran *et al.* 2003, Rajendran. 2003). Recent application of Photo Microscopy (3 D) further showed minute details of the skull bones and also identified three cervical vertebrae along with the skull (Fig. 8.2d). This confirmed the fact that the skull was not in detached condition rather it remained with the body in the matrix.

To bring out the micro features of the skull in detail Scanning Electron Microscopy (SEM) has been carried out under various magnifications ranging from hundred to fifteen thousand in 15 KV. It has unraveled several vital factors which were not identified earlier in the fossil study of the Middle Pleistocene antiquity (Fig. 8.3a-d, Fig. 8.4a). In order to make one to one comparison a recent human foetus has been examined under SEM and it has revealed features similar to those in the fossil (Fig. 8.4b-d).

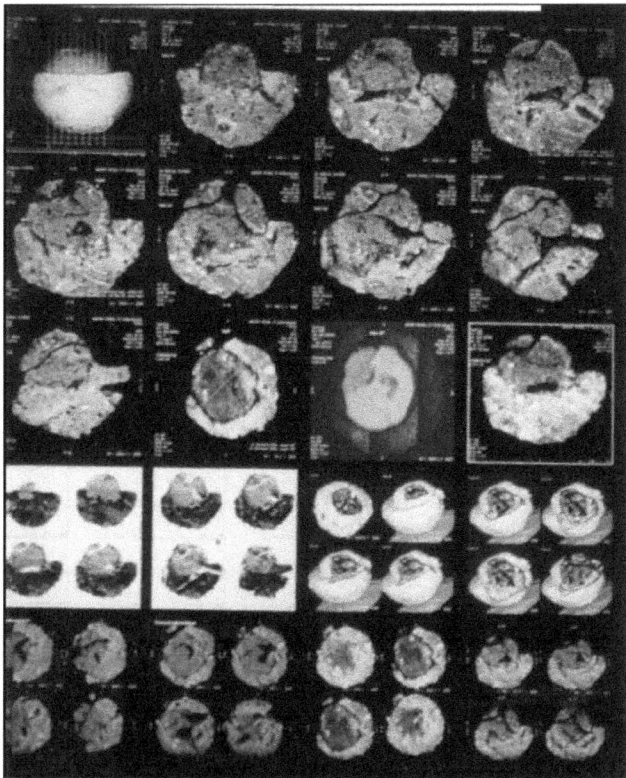

Fig. 8.2a. High resolution axial images
and 3D reformation

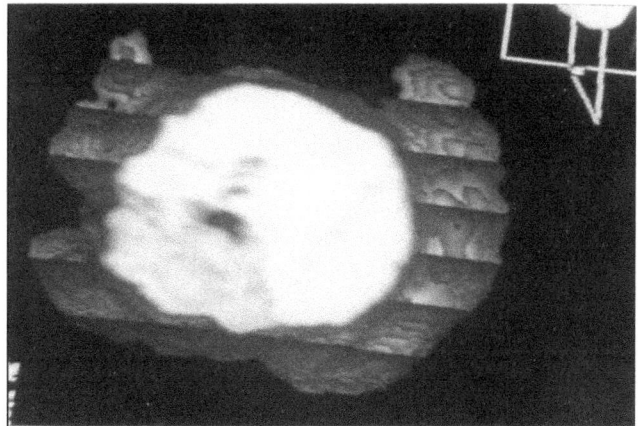

Fig. 8.2b. 3D minimum intensity projection
image of the skull

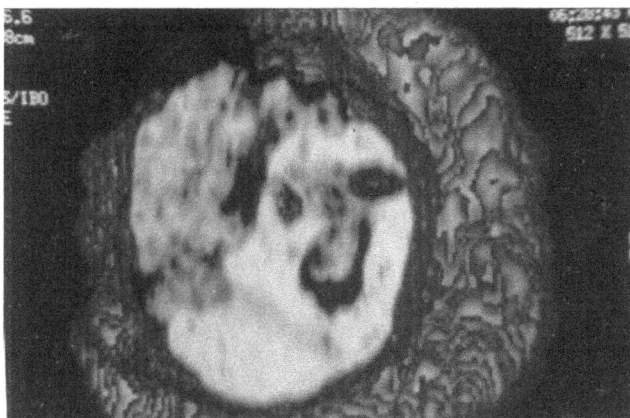

Fig. 8.2c. 3D minimum intensity projection
image of the face

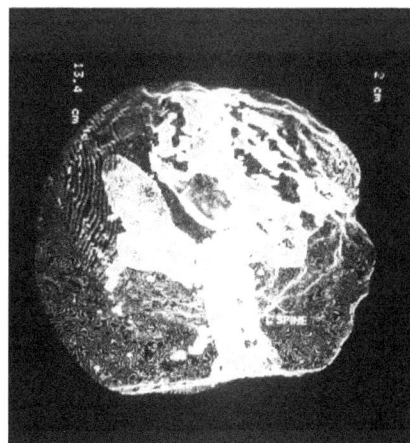

Fig. 8.2d. Identification of cervical vertebrae

DISCUSSION

In India most of the human remains from the archaeological contexts are found from the Mesolithic, Neolithic, Chalcolithic, and Megalithic cultural phases of the Holocene period. However, there are a few Palaeolithic sites in the country which have yielded Pleistocene human fossils, and they include the finds from Hathnora (Sonakia, 1998) and Bhimbetka (Wakankar. 1962, 1975., Misra *et al.* 1977., Kennedy *et al.* 1998) etc. The ferricrete at Odai is not implementiferous while the overlying non-ferricretised layers do contain Stone Age tools of the Upper Palaeolithic and Mesolithic cultures.

Utilization of the radiological methodology such as X-ray, 2 D, 3 D, Photo Microscopy (3 D) and SEM have helped to identify respectively the entombed fossil, cranium, complete skull along with fossilized brain tissues, teeth with in the gum, eyes with in the orbit, mandible, maxilla, three cervical vertebrae, bone structure, blood vessels, brain tissues, RBC, membranous tissue etc. The perfect shape and preservation of the fossilized RBC in pile of coins arrangement (Rouleux formation) is astonishing, and it is the same case with the blood vessels and brain tissues. Comparative study with the SEM images of a recent human foetus clearly established the human characteristics of the fossil.

63

Fig. 8.3a. Cranial bone structure & vessels

Fig. 8.3b. Vessels, Brain tissues & RBC

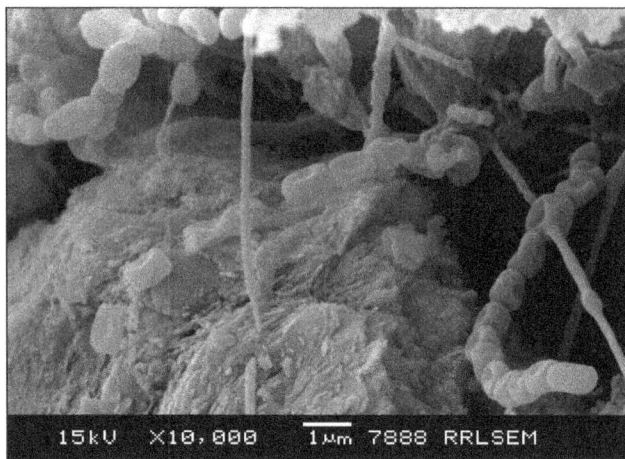

Fig. 8.3c. Dumbell shape of the RBC,
Bone structure & Vessels

Fig. 8.3d. Pile of coins arrangement
(ROULEUX FORMATION) of the RBC

CONCLUSION

It is for the first time a human fossil has been discovered within the ferricrete of the Middle Pleistocene and it has disproved the hypothesis that no organic remains stay within a deposit once the matrix undergoes ferricretization.

SEM study has unraveled several vital factors which were not identified earlier in the fossil study of greater antiquity. Pile of coins arrangement of the RBC and their clear revelation in dumbbell shape are important signatures identified through the SEM. Presence of the brain tissues, cranial bone structure and vessels in the fossilized skull, and identification of similar character-ristics in a recent cranium of a human foetus through the SEM are unique and remarkable. Images have proved the perfect nature of fossilization and preservation of the organic remains in its totality.

Since it is difficult to date fossilized organic matter, in this case the matrix which exactly covers over the skull has been dated by TL methodology. The date of 0.166 +/-

30 M obtained for the matrix approximately places the entombed fossil to the Middle Pleistocene (Rajendran *et al.* 2004). In the human evolutionary stage the Odai human fossil named 'Laterite Baby' belongs to the Homo sapiens (archaic). Based on the absolute dates of the human fossil evidences from India 'Laterite Baby' from Odai in Villupuram district of Tamil Nadu in South India is the Second Oldest one next to the Narmada fossil and is the first ever discovered human fossil within the ferricrete.

References

BRIGGS and CROWTHER. 2001. Palaeobiology II. Blackwell Scientific Publication.

KENNEDY. K.A.R. and A.A. ELGART.1998. Hominid remains: An Update South Asia. India and Sri Lanka. Belgium.

MISRA. V.N, Y. MATHPAL and M. NAGAR. 1977. Bhimbetka: Prehistoric Man and his art in Central India. Deccan College, Pune.

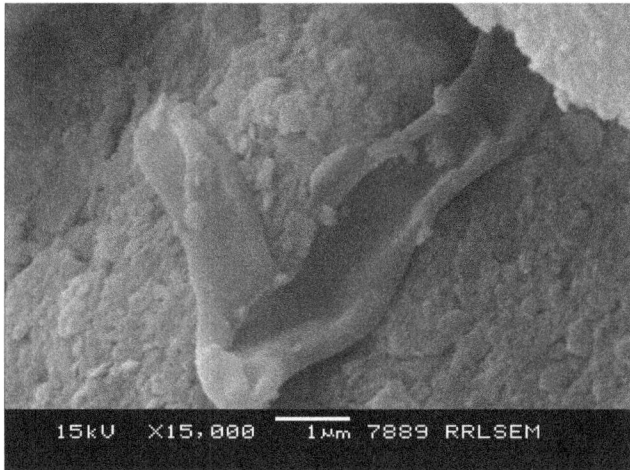

Fig. 8.4a. A distinct vessel section & Brain tissues

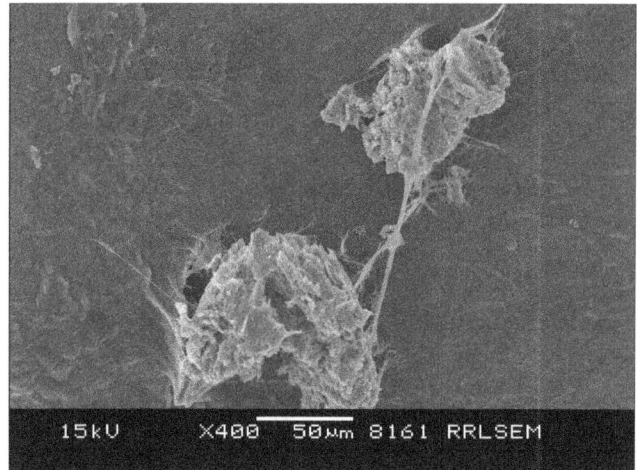

Fig. 8.4b. A Bone structure & the vessels

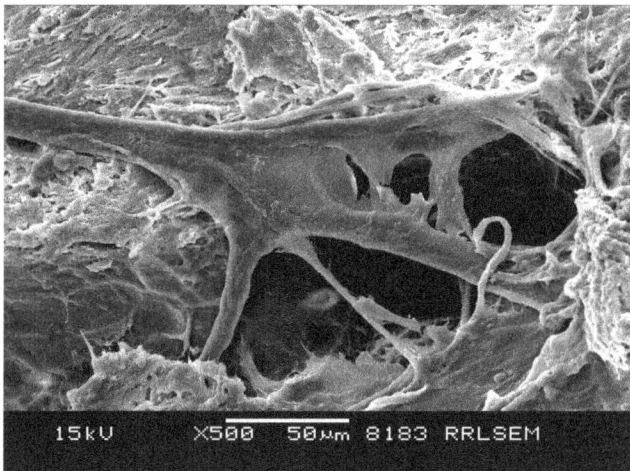

Fig. 8.4c. Vessels & Brain tissues

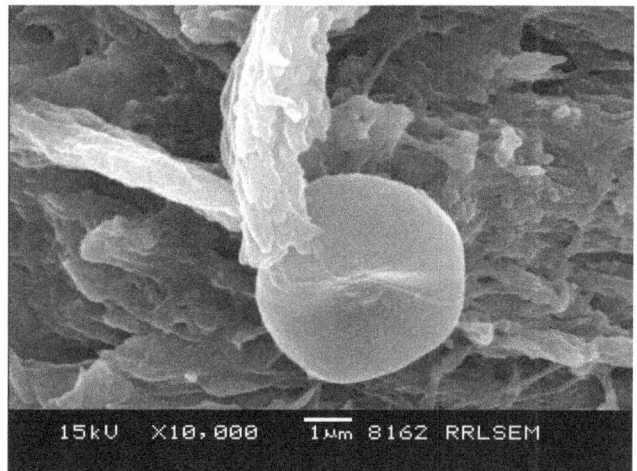

Fig. 8.4d. Distinct RBC in Dumbell shape, membranous tissue & Bone structure

RAJENDRAN, P. 2003. Unearthing India's Second Oldest human fossil. News India (Nature)-6:7. New Delhi.

RAJENDRAN. P, R. BHARATH KUMAR and B. VIJAYA BHANU. 2003. Fossilized hominid baby skull from the ferricrete at Odai, Bommayarpalayam, Villupuram District, Tamil Nadu, South India. Current Science- 84(6): 754-756. Bangalore.

RAJENDRAN. P, M.P. CHOUGAONKAR and C.S.P. IYER. 2004. Human baby skull within the Middle Pleistocene Ferricrete. Puratattva- 34: 1-4. New Delhi.

SONAKIA. A. 1998. Antiquity of the Narmada Homo erectus, the Early Man of India. Current Science- 75(4): 391-393. Bangalore.

WAKANKAR. V.S. 1962. Painted rock-shelter of India. Revista.di Science Prehistorische – 17: 132.

WAKANKAR. V.S. 1975. Bhimbetka the Pre-historic Paradise. Prachya Pratibha- 3(2): 7-29. Uttar Pradesh.

HUMAN BIO-CULTURAL DIVERSITY IN PREHISTORIC-TO-PROTOHISTORIC INDIA

A.R. SANKHYAN

Anthropological Survey of India, Indian Museum Campus,
27 Jawaharlal Nehru Road, Kolkata – 700016, India.
E-mail:sankhyan51@rediffmail.com

Abstract: Much of India's present-day diversity is due to hybridization among the intercontinental biological, ethnic, cultural and linguistic elements, which have entered into India from the west, north and Southeast Asia. Notwithstanding that, quite a significant portion of Indian ethnicity has its roots much deeper in the prehistoric past, though much of it has already been lost overtime, and could only be read in Indian prehistoric records. The present paper focuses more on this lost diversity, based on fossils and Palaeolithic industries. The fossil evidences from India take us much deeper in time to a pre-human era as well as to the earliest emergence of humans in South Asia. In sum, India provides a unique opportunity for those who wish to understand the bio-cultural basis of the diversity and unity of Indian ethos.
Keywords: India, bio-cultural, diversity, fossils, lithic industries

Résumé: Beaucoup de la diversité actuelle de l'Inde est due à une hybridation entre les éléments biologiques, éthniques, culturels et linguistiques intercontinentaux, lesquels entrèrent en Inde arrivés de l'Ouest, du Nord et du Sudest Asiatique. C'est pas surprenant qu'une partie significative de l'éthnicité Indienne ait ses racines très fond dans le passé préhistorique, même si beaucoup de ceci s'est déjà perdu au long du temps et ne peut plus être lu que dans les registres préhistoriques Indiens. Cet article porte attention sur la diversité perdue, sur la base de fossiles et d'industries Paléolithiques. Les évidences fossiles de l'Inde nous portent beaucoup plus profondément dans le temps, à un âge pré-humain ainsi qu'a la première émergence des humains en Asie du Sud. En somme, l'Inde offre une unique opportunité à ceux qui veulent comprendre les bases bio-culturelles de a diversité et de l'unité de l'ethos Indien.
Mots-clés: Inde, bio-culturel, diversité, fossiles, industries lithiques

INTRODUCTION

India is a vast land of complex biological and cultural entities. India's present-day biological and cultural diversity and socio-religious symbiosis owes its legacy to the prehistory and protohistory of the Indian sub-continent/ South Asia with extensions to Eurasia and Southeast Asia. The undeniable hard fossil evidences and ancient material cultures build a strong base to create a new scientific vision about our existence in time and space cutting across the continents, cultures and races. Therefore, Prehistory serves mankind in a very befitting way in the wake of increasing religious fundamentalism, ethic violence and traditional social/cultural orthodoxy or prejudices based on local legends, myths and superstitions.

In this paper the author has attempted a brief overview of the roots of Indian divergences and unities through a deep peep into the prehistory and protohistory based on fossil, skeletal, lithic and other cultural evidences. The paper endeavours to distinguish some of the threads of Indian past biological diversities from the complicated mess of the hard fossil and lithic cultural evidences including the recent genomic evidences. To account for the Indian prehistoric diversity, one may proceed chronologically as per the convention, starting from the earliest to the recent and may deal with the issues under three broad temporal frames: (1) Late Miocene-Pliocene, (2) Pleistocene to Early Holocene, and (3) Late Holocene/Protohistory.

OBSERVATIONS

Late Miocene – Pliocene (13-4 *mya*)

Africa has come out as the well-documented place of origin of the Early to Middle Miocene hominoids (Ape-like Ancestors) during the time bracket of 20-14 *mya* (million years ago) though hominoids had become very scarce during its Late Miocene. But, Europe, Eurasia and the Siwalik Hills of the Indian sub-continent, e.g., the sub-Himalayan region of Northwest was the golden period of the Late Miocene antecedents of man during 13 to 5 *mya*. Indian Early hominoids have global implications since they were highly diversified and included the common ape-human ancestors- the "ape-men" (hominoids) and "man-apes" or "half-humans" (Plio-Pleistocene hominids). In Siwaliks, for instance, one medium sized hominoid- *Ramapithecus*- was widely regarded the earliest representative of the human family, and the large one, *Sivapithecus* as that of the Asian great ape- the Orangutan, and another, the *Krishnapithecus (similar to European Pliopithecus),* was the ancestor of the Gibbons. These hominoids ranged in time from 12.3 *mya* (Kappelman *et al.*, 1991) to 5.5 *mya* (Sankhyan, 1985)- a very crucial period during which the hominoid-hominid divergence had occurred. Although, palaeoanthropologists recently hotly debated the status of the Siwalik hominoids and some also lump *Ramapithecus* with *Sivapithecus,* it still retains a specific distinction within the latter as a species, thereby making *Sivapithecus* as a highly diversified group constituting at least four species:

1. Largest: *S. parvada* (extinct species)

2. Large: *S. indicus* (likely ancestral to the Orangutan)

3. Medium: *S. punjabicus = S. sivalensis (=Ramapithecus*: akin to hominids)

4. Smallest: *S. simonsi* (probably an extinct European migrant of *Dryopithecus*).

Along with these hominoids, the Siwaliks had another very giant hominoid- the *Gigantopithecus bilaspurensis*-believed to still existing in the remote corners of the Himalayas as the legendary "Yet" ("Himalayan Snow Man"). The author (ARS) has made several reviews on these hominoids (Sankhyan, 1988, 1990, 1998, 2005), and concludes that Siwalik hominoids still hold a key in understanding the Last Common Ancestor of the hominids and the great apes, which sounds something like *"up from the hominid and not from the ape"*.

Pleistocene to Early Holocene (2mya-5kya)

Fossil Evidences

The Pleistocene (2 mya to10 kya) of India is well known for the Palaeolithic cultural diversities. There were many distinct lithic cultural traditions in the Stone Age- right from the Lower Palaeolithic through the Middle and Upper Palaeolithic to Mesolithic and Neolithic, which could be associated with different waves of humanity. But, the hominin biological entities responsible for their creation are poorly understood due to the recovery of very meagre fossil evidences. The documented Pleistocene biological event in India goes back only to the Middle Pleistocene- around half a million years ago recorded in the Central Narmada Valley. The discovery of a fossilized partial Skullcap (Sonakia, 1984) and three postcranial fossils- a complete right and a partial left clavicle (collarbone) and of a 9th left thoracic rib (Sankhyan 1997 a & b, 2005) reveal the existence of at least two different kinds of early humans inhabiting Central /Peninsular India:

i. **The "archaic" *Homo sapiens*-** represented by the skull. It was a heavily muscled man with large brain (#1250cc), drawing closer to the European ante-Neanderthals (Kennedy & Chiment, 1991, Kennedy, 2000: Cameron *et al.*, 2005). A minority of palaeoanthropologists also considers it as an "evolved" *H. erectus* (M. – A. Lumley & Sonakia, 1985) based on grade concept.

ii. **The "Robust / archaic Pygmy"-** represented by the postcranial fossils. As revealed by the fossils attributable to an adult female, its body scaled to a modern Pygmy with very short body dimensions, viz., the stature (about 135 cm) and upper shoulder diameter (about 30cm), but it was very robust and archaic (Sankhyan, 2005). It would not be surprise to guess the existence of very small hominins in Narmada Valley half a million years ago if we recall the late survival of tiny early humans having lived beside the modern humans in Indonesian island of Flores, and known as "Hobbits"- a different species of man- the *Homo floresiensis*.

Lithic Cultural Evidences

The Narmada human fossils are associated with well-refined Late Acheulian bifaces, cleavers, choppers, besides the Middle Palaeolithic discoidal cores and scrapers also recovered from the same stratigraphic horizon (H. de Lumley & Sonakia, 1985, Bhattacharya & Sonakia, 1989, Badam *et al.*, 1986, Sankhyan, 1997 a, b).

The Acheulian Man: Indian Acheulian in general shows some differences (Pappu, 2001, 2002), yet it is technologically similar to the Old World (African and European) Acheulian (McPherron, 2000; Noll and Petraglia, 2003). These are however, distributed sparsely and found in buried contexts (Mishra, 1994, Mishra *et al.*, 1995) but so far have yielded no associated fossil evidence. The Early Acheulians in South Asia is apparently of the Lower Pleistocene age- probably representing the earliest human migration to South Asia. The Late Acheulian sites are found in preponderance in surface contexts (Pappu, 2001) and are mostly restricted to the Middle and Upper Pleistocene and show intense hominin activity during the Middle Pleistocene as documented by the fossil evidence recovered at Hathnora in Central Narmada Valley. The Late Acheulian (inclusive of the Middle Acheulian), sometimes also referred to as 'transitional' (Jayaswal, 1978, 1982), has a greater artefact density and overall distributional pattern throughout the Indian subcontinent. We encounter these sites in a variety of geomorphological contexts and ecological settings. Some important reported examples are found in the studies of de Terra and Paterson (1939), Khatri (1966), Joshi (1985), Joshi *et al.* (1974), Allchin & Chakrabarti (1979), Armand (1985), Jacobson (1985), Misra (1985, 1989, 1995, 1998, 2001), Misra and Mate (1995), Chakrabarti (1988), Reddy *et al.* (1995), Paddyya (1987, 1994), Paddayya *et al.* (2002), Clark (1998), Chattopadhyaya *et al.* (2002), Varma (1997), Chauhan (2003), etc.

The Late Acheulian could have been partly the product of local evolution from early Acheulian and partly due to immigration to the sub-continent. Separation of the Indian Late Acheulian (Lower Palaeolithic) from the Middle Palaeolithic is a major problem (Jayaswal, 1974; 1978, Mishra, 1995), but compared to the Lower Palaeolithic types, these could be distinguished by a decrease in size of the artifacts, their refinement, addition of some specialized tools made on fine-grained raw material, like chert, jasper, chalcedony, flint, crypto-crystalline silica, etc. based on the prepared-core technique, accountable to a distinct shift in human mobility marked by changes in land-use. They are generally found near sources of raw material, such as gravel or conglomerate beds and within sandy-pebbly gravel horizons; generally overlying the basal boulder gravels comprising Lower Palaeolithic artifacts (Guzder, 1980). The diminutive choppers and handaxes of the Middle Palaeolithic (Guzder, 1980; Tewari *et al.*, 2002; Corvinus, 2002) could be pointers of a divide between the 'light-duty' assemblages of the Middle Palaeolithic and the 'heavy-duty' assemblages of the Lower Palaeolithic. We may also visualise a local evolution of the former from the latter.

The Soanian Man: Mohapatra (1981, 1990, 2006) viewed a remarkable individuality of the Soanian unlike other pebble-cobble tool cultures, and noted that it flourished through three successive evolutionary stages- Early, Late and Evolved / Final Soan, spanning the period from Middle Pleistocene to Early Holocene. All Soanian evidences come from post-Siwalik contexts excepting one claimed of the Lower Pleistocene or earlier age from the Potwar region in Pakistan (Rendell & Dennel, 1985; Dennell, 2003). The early Soanian is certainly of non-biface character (*contra* Acheulian biface) as the basic typo-technological distinctiveness. Yet, the Acheulian in the sub-Himalayas is enigmatic because of its limited or sporadic and very sparse occurrence, that too in the Frontal Range only, unlike the Soanian having wider distribution spanning the major part of the Pleistocene and appearing more vigorous and prolific than the Acheulian. Nowhere have the artefacts of the two cultures been recorded together in reliably stratified *in situ* contexts. Also, from typo-technological point of view there appears to be no link between the two cultures. For instance, while the Soanian specialized in working on cobbles (64 to 256 mm diameters), the Acheulian artefacts were made from boulders (over 256 mm diameter). It is likely that the Acheulian exclusively found in the Range area could have reached the sub-Himalayan terrain only towards the end of the Pleistocene. The Soanian occurring on the Middle Pleistocene terraces (T1 and T2), flourished in a different ecosystem that was older and more stable and had hominized the region much vigorously earlier that the Acheulian.

Genomic Evidences

Genomic Evidences pertain to the anatomically modern *Homo sapiens* only. Rao and Chandrasekar in their latest review (2006) indicate that the most ancient mtDNA haplotypes are L1, L2 and L3, among them L1 and L2 are specific to sub-Saharan Africa. It is the L3 – with its lineages M and N that have come out of Africa and colonized Asia and Europe during 50-70 *kya*. M haplotype has come likely via the southern route and spread further eastward. The Indian specific sub-clades are U2, M2 and R5, and also the most ancient (50-70 *kya*). Among these M2 is the oldest (70.6±21*kya*) and is frequently found in the Dravidian speakers (9-13 %), with a moderate frequency in the Indo-European speakers (3-5%) and the least frequency in the Austro-Asiatic groups (0.7 to 8 %). Another most common sub-clade of N is R, especially the R5, but absent in the Austro-Asiatics. Another very common haplogroup is U, which is very common among North Indian Muslims (> 30%), followed

by Hindu castes (15–20%), and the tribes (10%), but missing in the Mongoloids. It is regarded as the second migration out of Africa, especially from Ethiopia during the Late Pleistocene.

Indian populations have significant representations of the U1 and U7, but their U2i sub-haplogroup is highest in the tribes, who interestingly, almost entirely lack the U2e-characteristic of the West Eurasians and also common in Indian upper castes. The time estimated for the split between Indian and the Western-Eurasian U2 lineages is 53±4 *kya*. This date is close to the time suggested for the peopling of Asia and first expansion of the anatomically modern humans in Europe.

Speculating the General Stone Age Scenario

Notwithstanding, the paucity of fossils, we may still visualise at least two different species of the early hominins through the cultural traditions of the Lower Palaeolithic of India / Indian sub-continent. There could have been many distinct populations of the anatomically modern *Homo sapiens* in the rest of the Stone Age since, in general, with the addition of a new biological population we encounter addition of new cultural change. We visualise the following scenario of the population diversity on the basis of the various cultures of the Stone Age of India:

1. *Homo erectus* populations as the creators of the Soanian Cultural traditions of the Sub-Himalayas.

2. Another*Homo erectus* population as the creator of the Early Acheulian Cultural tradition of the Peninsular India.

3. "Archaic" *Homo sapiens* populations as the authors of the Late Acheulian-to- Middle Palaeolithic Cultural traditions of the Peninsular India.

4. Probably a different "archaic" *Homo sapiens* as the author of the Middle Palaeolithic tradition of the Sub-Himalayas.

5. Several populations of the anatomically modern *Homo sapiens* as the authors of the Upper Palaeolithic traditions of the Peninsular India, the Sub-Himalayas and the Hoabinhinian and Upper Annyathian Culture of the North-eastern India; the latter arrived from Burma / South East Asia.

6. Several populations of the Mesolithic hunter-gatherers in Peninsular and North India, some having evolved locally besides the immigrants.

7. At least two different waves of the modern *Homo sapiens* humanity that created the Neolithic culture in the Northwest and the Northeast.

Late Holocene/Proto-history (5 –3 *kya*)

The Chalcolithic Indians

The Chalcolithic and the Bronze Age populations, followed by the Iron Age Megalithic builders of India, primarily dominate this period. The Chalcolithic and the Bronze Age populations were mostly confined to the Northwest and Southwest India, whereas the Iron Age Megalithic populations were distributed in two primary pockets- one in the North-eastern and the other in the Southern India, and represent different biological populations.

India has been the land of most ancient civilizations in the world; we are all familiar with the Harappan or Indus civilization, recently also referred to as 'Indus-Saraswati' civilization that was contemporaneous to, and shared many harmonious linkages with other famous civilizations- the Greek, Nile and Mesopotamia over 5000 years ago. From the genomic standpoint, Rao and Chandrasekar (2006) have observed, "only a small fraction of the Caucasoid-specific mtDNA lineages is found in Indian populations ascribed to a relatively recent admixture, equated with Indo-Aryan "invasion" about 4000 years ago. Genetic distances indicate that Tibeto-Burman speaking tribal population of eastern India is more closely related to the Asians than to other Indians, but Indian caste populations are more closely related to the Europeans than to the Eastern Asians". In the light of various studies [T.C. Sharma (1966, 1991), O.K. Singh & T.C. Sharma (1969), H.C. Sharma (1972), Sankalia (1981), Ramesh (1986), M.J. Singh (1991), etc.], we may visualize the Late Holocene population scenario of India as follows:

1. At least three different waves of the modern *Homo sapiens* humanity during the Chalcolthic and Bronze Age of the Northwest and the Southwestern / Peninsular India.

2. At least two different waves of the modern *Homo sapiens* humanity as authors of the Megalithic cultures of the Peninsular and Northeast India.

3. At least two different waves of modern *Homo sapiens* humanity for the Iron Age culture of the Northwest / North India- the *Aryans*.

The Bronze Age Harappans

The proto-historic urban centres of Indian civilization were first discovered in 1920s at Harappa and Mohen-jo-daro in Indus Valley. Since then over 85 sites have been discovered in the Indus Valley, and manifold so in India, about 1500 sites, extending even beyond the Yamuna in the east. But, most of the major sites are concentrated along the lost legendary river Saraswati, hence gained a new *nomen*, the *Indus-Saraswati Civilization* [Gupta (1997), Joshi (2001), Kenoyer (1998) Lal (1997)]. This civilization is one of the three great early civilizations that arose in the late fourth and third millennia BC around the three large alluvial systems of the Tigris-Euphrates, Nile and Indus rivers.

Biological Diversity & Affinities

The Skeletal biology suggests that the Harappans are most close to the ancient people of the ancient Mesopotamia and Sumer- ancient Iraq, Iran and Turkey, besides Egypt (Dutta, 1983; Gupta *et al.*, 1962; Kennedy, 2000; Lukacs, 1976, 1984). In other words they form a common gene pool with the ancient people of the Middle East, but had considerable regional diversity. Following findings emerge from the craniometrical, non-metric and dental studies

1. That the mature Harappans belonged to at least Five population Types (which also include the proto-australoid and mongoloid populations):

   A: Tall-robust-long head – broad nose (Cemetery R37).

   A1: Short-gracile-long head-medium nose (Cemetery R37 & Area G).

   A2: Medium (height, head and nose)-low face (Cemetery H: Stratum I).

   B1: Short-round-headed-long nosed (Area G).

   B2: Tall-round headed-long nose (Cemetery H: Stratum II).

2. That more than one type is found together: The cemetery H: Stratum-I represented four (A-B1) types; cemetery H: stratum-II had three (A-A1, B2) types; Area G had two (A-A1) types.

3. That in the head shape, the Indus people are closer to their extant geographical populations: the Harappan-closer to the Punjabis, the Mohen-jo-daro- closer to the Sindhi, and the Lothal – closer to the Gujarati.

4. That despite of the shared biological affinities, the Indus people were also unique and had indigenous origins among the Pre-Harappans- the Kot Diji, Amri, Kalibangan, etc.

5. That there is no skeletal evidence of the so-called massacre through metal weapons

Cultural Diversity & Affinities:

There are a number of studies, to name few, e.g., Allchin and Allchin (1968, 1982), Thapar (1973), Gupta (1997), Joshi (2001), Kenoyer (1998) Lal (1997), etc., which discuss the archaeological / cultural history, diversity and affinities of the Harappan people. We may summarize these as follows:

1. *Trade Linkages*: Unto Sutkagen Dor (Baluchistan) beyond Iran, which was once on a navigable inlet of the Arabian Sea and on the trade route from the famous Lothal dockyard to Mesopotamia-Evident from a) the presence of Indus seals at Ur and other Mesopotamian cities, and the 'Persian Gulf'- type of seals at Lothal; b) the standard weights of the Harappans reveal them as great traders- exported cotton textiles, ivory and copper.

2. *Occupational Linkages*: Besides the traders and the ruling class and the priests, the Harappans were

occupationally diversified. Had excellent craftsmen-potters/terracotta specialists, bead makers, and metal utensil makers in copper, bronze, lead and tin, and masons; there were also cultivator and pastoral groups.

3. *Linguistic Linkages*: Harappans inscriptions place them distant from the Indo-European, Sumerian, Hurrian, Elamite and the Mundari, but draw closer to the Dravidian (esp. the Old Tamil- akin to the Brahui of Baluchistan). This likely indicates indigenous origins from the Pre-Harappans.

4. *Religious Linkages*: The Harappa religion shows similarities with the old Dravidian cultural elements of Hinduism in: (i) the cult of the *Great Mother Goddess* of the Ancient Near East- evident from Harappan female figurines and seals in association with the sacred *pipal* tree, (ii) a *three-faced male god* (Yogi), (iii) the existence of the *priest*, (iv) the common practice of the disposal of the dead by inhumation and burring with grave offerings, (v) the ceremonial bathing in the Great Bath of Mohen-jo-daro, carried out in the small antechambers adjoining the bath- probably as a prelude to a ritual cohabitation with the dancing women associated with the goddess. The Harappan seems to be a tolerant society.

The Harappan urban centre is thought to have declined gradually with eastward spread in different pockets unto the Yamua River or even beyond unto the Ganges. Different workers assign different reasons for the decline and the mains causes could have been as follows:

1. *Overpopulation*: Due to intruders (c.1750 B.C.)- Evident from changes in pottery- from finer to coarse; divisions of large rooms.

2. *Internal decay and flooding*: Led to gradual deserting of the township due to less maintenance of the streets, drainage system, etc.

3. *An eastward movement*- evident from the fact that the Harappan sites towards central and southern India flourished after the decline of Harappa and Mohen-jo-daro cities.

4. *"Aryan Invasion"*: There is no specific evidence of mass destruction by the RgVedic Aryans; there was no *"eclipse or collapse"*. But, of late, the chariot riding peoples (Aryans) were wide spread in the 2nd millennium B.C., e.g., during King Solomon's reign over Israel (970-931 B.C.); the chariots and horses were imported from Egypt to the Asia Minor.

References

ALLCHIN, B. and F. R. ALLCHIN. 1968. The Birth of Indian Civilization: India and Pakistan before 500 B.C. Harmondsworth: Penguin.

ALLCHIN, B. and F. R. ALLCHIN. 1982. The rise of a Civilization: The Prehistory and Earl History of South Asia. New Delhi: Viking Penguin Books.

ALLCHIN, F.R. and D.K CHAKRABARTI (Editors). 1979. A Source book of Indian Archaeology. Delhi: Munshiram Manoharlal Publihers Pvt. Ltd.

ARMAND, J. 1985. "The emergence of the handaxe tradition in Asia, with special reference to India." In Recent Advances in Indo-Pacific Prehistory. Edited by V.N. Misra and P. Bellwood, pp. 3-8. New Delhi: Oxford & IBH Publishing Co.

BADAM, G.L., R.K. GANJOO, R.K.G. SALAHUDDIN, and S.N. RAJAGURU. 1986. Evolution of fossil hominin – the maker of Late Acheulian tools at Hathnora, Madhya Pradesh, India. Current Science **55** (3): 143 – 145.

BHATTACHARYA, D.K. and A. SONAKIA. 1989. "Cultural remains from the earliest hominid site on Narmada". In Changing Perspectives of Anthropology in India. Edited by S.C. Tiwari, pp. 313 – 320. New Delhi: Today and Tomorrow's Printers and Publishers.

CAMERON, D., R. PATNAIK and A. SAHNI. 2005. The phylogenic significance of the Middle Pleistocene Narmada hominin cranium from Central India. International Journal of Osteoarchaeology

CHAKRABARTI, D.K. 1988. A History of Indian Archaeology – From the Beginning to 1947. New Delhi: Munshiram Manoharlal Publishers Pvt. Ltd.

CHATTOPADHYAYA, I., B. VIKRAMA and S. VIKRAMA. 2002. "A survey of prehistoric investigations by the Archaeological Survey of India since Independence." Appendix. In Indian Archaeology in Retrospect: The Archaeology of Early India. Edited by S. Settar and R. Korisettar. Delhi: Manohar Publishers, Appendix.

CHAUHAN, P.R. 2003. An Overview of the Siwalik Acheulian & Reconsidering its Chronological Relationship with the Soanian – A Theoretical Perspective. Assemblage 7.

CLARK, J.D. 1998. "The Early Palaeolithic of the eastern region of the Old World in comparison to the West." In Early Human Behaviour in Global Context: the Rise and Diversity of the Lower Palaeolithic Record. Edited by M. Petraglia and R. Korisettar, pp. 437-450. New York: Routledge Press.

CORVINUS, G. 2002. Arjun 3, a Middle Palaeolithic Site, in the Deokhuri Valley, Western Nepal. Man and Environment XXVII (2), 31-44.

DENNELL, R.W. 2003. Dispersal and colonization, long and short chronologies: how continuous is the Early Pleistocene record for hominids outside East Africa? Journal of Human Evolution 45, 421-440.

DE TERRA, H. and T.T. PATERSON. 1939. Studies on the Ice Age in India and Associated Human Cultures. Washington D.C.: Carnegie Institute Publication 493.

DUTTA, P.C. 1983. The Bronze Age Harappans. Calcutta: Anthropological Survey of India.

GUPTA, P.P., P.C. DUTTA and A. BASU. 1962. Human Remains from Harappa. Calcutta: Anthropological Survey of India.

GUPTA, S.P. 1997. The Indus-Saraswati Civilization. New Delhi: Pratibha Prakshan.

GUZDER, S. 1980. Quaternary Environment and Stone Age Cultures of the Konkan (Coastal Maharashtra, India). Pune: Deccan College Postgraduate and Research Institute.

HEMPHILL, B.E. J.R. LUKACS and K.A.R. KENNEDY. 1991. Biological adaptations and affinities of Bronze Age Harappans. In Harappan Excavations 1986-1990: A Multidisciplinary Approach to Third millennium Urbanism. Ed.. R.H. Meadow, pp137-182. Madison: Prehistory Press.

JACOBSON, J. 1985. "Acheulian surface sites in Central India." In Recent Advances in Indo-Pacific Prehistory. Edited by V.N. Misra and P. Bellwood, pp.49-57. New Delhi: Oxford & IBH Publishing Co.

JAYASWAL, V. 1974. "A techno-typological review of the Middle Palaeolithic cultures of India." Puratattva 7, 12-16.

JAYASWAL, V. 1978. Palaeohistory of India – A Study of the Prepared Core Technique. New Delhi: Agam Kala Prakashan.

JAYASWAL, V. 1982. Chopper-Chopping Component of Palaeolithic India. Delhi: Agam Kala Prakashan.

JOSHI, JAGATPATI. 2001. Harappan Civilization as seen at the Close of the Twentieth Century in M&E XXV (1). Poona

JOSHI, R.V. 1985. "The characteristics of the Pleistocene climatic events in India Sub-continent – A land of monsoon climate." In Studies in Indian Archaeology. Edited by S.B. Deo and M.K. Dhavalikar, pp. 53-63. Bombay: Popular Prakashan,

JOSHI, R.V., S.N. RAJAGURU, R.S. PAPPU and B.P. BOPARDIKAR. 1974. Quaternary glaciations and Palaeolithic sites in the Liddar Valley (Jammu-Kashmir). World Archaeology 5 (3), 369-79.

KAPPELMAN, J., KELLEY, J., PILBEAM, D.R., SHEIKH, K.A., WARD, S., ANWAR, M., BARRY, J.C., BROWN, B., HAKE, P., JOHNSON, N.M., RAZA, S.M., and S.M. I. SHAH. 1991. The earliest occurrence of Sivapithecus from the middle Miocene Chinji Formation of Pakistan. J. Human Evolution 21: 61–73.

KENOYER J.M. 1998. Ancient Cities of the Indus Valley Civilization. Karachi: Oxford University Press and the American institute of Pakistan Studies.

KENNEDY, K.A.R. 2000. God-Apes and Fossil Men – Palaeoanthropology of South Asia. Ann Arbor: University of Michigan Press.

KENNEDY, K.A.R. and J. CHIMENT. 1991 "The fossil hominid from the Narmada valley, India: Homo erectus or Homo sapiens?" In Indo-Pacific Prehistory.

Edited by P. Bellwood, pp. 42-58. Canberra: Indo-Pacific Prehistory Association,.

KHATRI, A.P. 1966. "Origin and evolution of hand-axe culture in the Narmada Valley (Central India)." In Studies in Prehistory (Robert Bruce Foote Memorial Volume). Edited by D. Sen and A.K. Ghosh, pp. 96-121. Calcutta: Firma K.L. Mukhopadhyay,.

LAL, B.B. 1997. The Earliest Civilization of South Asia: Rise, Maturity and Decline. New Delhi: Aryan Books International

LUKACS, J.R. 1976. Dental anthropology and the biological affinities of an Iron Age population from Pomparippu, Srilanka. In Ecological Backgrounds of South Asian Prehistory, ed. K.A.R. Kennedy and G.L. Possehl, 197-215. South Asia Occasional Papers and Theses, South Asia Program, Cornel University, 1th Aca. 4.

LUKACS, J.R. 1984. Dental anthropology of South Asian populations: A review. In The People of South Asia: Biological Anthropology of India, Pakistan, and Nepal. Ed. J.R. Lukacs, pp. 133-157. New York: Plenum Press.

LUMLEY, H. DE and A. SONAKIA. 1985. Contexte stratigraphique et Archaeologique de L'Homme de le Narmada, Hathnora, Madhya Pradesh, Inde. L'Anthropologie **89**: 3 – 12.

LUMLEY, M.-A. and A. SONAKIA. 1985. Premiere de coaverte d'un Homo erectus sur le continent Indien A. Hathnora, dans la Moyenne Vallee de la Narmada. L'Anthropologie 89: 13 – 61.

McPHERRON, S.P. 2000. Handaxes as a measure of the mental capabilities of early hominids. Journal of Archaeological Science 27, 655–663.

MISHRA, S. 1994. "The South Asian Lower Palaeolithic." Man and Environment XIX (1-2), 57-72.

MISHRA, S. 1995. "Chronology of the Indian Stone Age: the impact of recent Absolute and relative dating attempts". Man and Environment, XX (2), 11-16.

MISHRA, S., VENKATESAN, T.R., and B.L.K. SOMAYAJULU. 1995."Earliest Acheulian industry from Peninsular India". Current Anthropology 36 (5), 847-51.

MISRA, V.N. 1985. "The Acheulian succession at Bhimbetka." In Recent Advances in Indo-Pacific Prehistory. Edited by V.N. Misra and P. Bellwood, pp. 35-47. Oxford & IBH Publishing Co.

MISRA, V.N. 1989. "Stone Age India: An ecological perspective." Man and Environment XIV, 17-64.

MISRA, V.N. 1995. "Geoarchaeology of the Thar Desert, Northwest India." In Quaternary Environments and Geoarchaeolgy of India. Edited by S. Wadia, R. Korisettar and V.S. Kale, pp. 210-230. Bangalore: Geological Society of India.

MISRA, V.N. 1998. "Middle Pleistocene adaptations in India." In The Pleistocene Old World- Regional

Perspectives. Edited by O. Soffer, pp. 99-119. New York: Plenum Press,

MISRA, V.N. 2001. Prehistoric human colonization of India. Journal of Bioscience 26 (4), 491-531.

MISRA, V.N. and M.S. MATE (Editors). 1995. Indian Prehistory: 1964. Pune: Deccan College Post-graduate and Research Institute.

MOHAPATRA, G.C. 1981. Acheulian discoveries in the Siwalik Frontal Range. Current Anthropology 22 (4): 433-435.

MOHAPATRA, G.C., 1990, On the track of Early Man in western sub-Himalayas, Presidential Address at the 77th session of the Indian Science Congress, Anthropology and Archaeology Section, Cochin.

NOLL, M. and M.D. PETRAGLIA. 2003. "Acheulean bifaces and early human behavioural patterns in East Africa and South India." In Multiple Approaches to the Study of Bifacial Technologies. Edited by M. Soressi and Dibble, pp. 31-53. Philadelphia: University of Pennsylvania Press.

PADDAYYA, K. 1987. "The place of the study of site formation processes in prehistoric research in India." In Natural Formation Processes and the Archaeological Record. Edited by D.T. Nash and M.D. Petraglia, pp. 74-85. BAR International Series 352,.

PADDAYYA, K. 1994. "Investigation of man-environment relationships in Indian archaeology: Some theoretical considerations." Man and Environment, XIX (1-2), 1-28.

PADDAYYA, K., B.A.B. BLACKWELL, R. JHALDI-YAL, M.D. PETRAGLIA, S. FEVRIER, S., D.A. CHADERTON II, J.I.B. BLICKSTEIN, and A.R. SKINNER. 2002. Recent findings on the Acheulian of the Hunsgi and Baichbal valleys, Karnataka, with special reference to the Isampur excavation and its dating. Current Science 83 (5), 641–647.

PAPPU, R.S. 2001. Acheulian Culture in Peninsular India. New Delhi: D.K. Printworld (P) Ltd.

PAPPU, R.S. 2002. "The Lower Palaeolithic culture of India." In Recent Studies in India Archaeology. Edited by K. Paddayya, pp. 17-59. New Delhi: Munshiram Manoharlal Publishers Pvt. Ltd.,

RAO V.R. and A. CHANDRASEKAR. 2006. Genetic Finger Printing and Peopling of Indian sub-Continent. In "Human Origins in India: Genomic, dental, palaeontological and archaeological Evidence". Edited by V.R. Rao and A.R. Sankhyan (In Press).

REDDY, K.T., P.V. PRAKASH, A. RATH and CH.U.B. RAO, 1995. A Pebble tool assemblage on the Visakhapatnam Coast. Man and Environment XX (1): 113-118.

RAMESH, N.R. 1986. Discovery of Stone Age tools from Tripura and its relevance to the prehistory of South East Asia. GEOSEA V Proceedings, Vol. II, Geol. Soc. Malaysia, Bull. 20:289-310.

RENDELL, H. and R.W. DENNELL. 1985, Dated Lower Palaeolithic artifacts. Current Anthropology. 26 (3): 393.

SANKALIA, H.D. 1981. From history to Prehistory in Assam. In: Cultural Contours of India (Ed. V.S. Srivastava), pt II. Abhinav Publications.

SANKHYAN, A.R. 1985. Late occurrence of Sivapithecus in Indian Siwaliks. J. Human Evolution 14: 573-578.

SANKHYAN, A.R. 1988. On human ancestry: A new perspective. In Current Anthropological and Archaeological Perspectives. K.L. Bhowmik (ed.), Vol.-I, Man. New Delhi: Inter-India Publication, pp. 57-88.

SANKHYAN, A.R. 1990. A Re-thinking on the 'Human Great Ape' cladogenesis and the last common ancestor. Journal Anthropological Survey of India 39: 169-190.

SANKHYAN, A.R. 1997a. Fossil Clavicle of a Middle Pleistocene hominin from the Central Narmada Valley, India. Journal of Human Evolution (London) 32: 3-16.

SANKHYAN, A.R. 1997b. A new human fossil find from the Central Narmada basin and its chronology. Current Science 73 (12): 1110-1111.

SANKHYAN, A.R. 1998. A Re-appraisal of the Phylogenetic status of the Neogene Hominoids in human ancestry: In V. Bhalla Festchrift Volume (Ed. I. J. S. Jaiswal) Physical Anthropology & Human Genetics: Contemporary Perspectives, Ludhiana: Asia Vision, pp 128-146.

SANKHYAN, A.R. 1999. "The place of Narmada hominin in the Jigsaw puzzle of human origins". In Quaternary of India. Edited by M.P. Tiwari and D.M. Mohabey, pp. 335-345 Gondvana Geological Magazine Spl. Publ.

SANKHYAN, A.R. 2005. New fossils of Early Stone Age man from central Narmada Valley. Current Science 88 (5): 704-707.

SHARMA, H.C. 1972. Stone Age Culture of Garo Hills. Ph.D Thesis, Gauhati University.

SHARMA, T.C. 1966. Prehistoric archaeology of Assam-A study of Neolithic Culture, PhD Thesis, London University.

SHARMA, T.C. 1991. Prehistoric situation in North East India. In: Archaeology of North-eastern India (Eds. J.P. Singh & G. Sengupta), pp.41-58.Vikash Publishing House Pvt.Ltd., New Delhi.

SINGH, M.J. 1991. Prehistory of Manipur. In: Archaeology of North-eastern India (Eds. J. P. Singh & G. Sengupta), pp.126-130.Vikash Publishing House Pvt.Ltd., New Delhi.

SINGH, O.K. and T.C. SHARMA. 1969. On the discovery of Stone Age relics from Manipur. Journal of Assam Science Society 12:36-48.

SONAKIA, A. 1984. The Skull Cap of Early Man and associated mammalian fauna from Narmada Valley Alluvium, Hoshangabad area, M.P. (India). Records Geological Survey of India 113:159-172.

TEWARI, R., P.C. PANT, I.B. SINGH, S. SHARMA, M. SHARMA, P. SRIVASTAVA, A.K. SINGHVI, P.K. MISHRA and H.J. TOBSCHALL. 2002. Middle Palaeolithic human activity and palaeoclimate at Kalpi in Yamuna Valley, Ganga Plain. Man and Environment XXVII (2), 1-13.

THAPAR, B.K. 1973. New traits of the Indus civilization at Kalibangan: An appraisal. In South Asian Archaeology. Ed. N. Hammond, pp. 85-104. London: Duckworth.

VARMA, R. 1997. Prehistoric research in India: An assessment. Man and Environment XXII (1), 1-7.

IS STUDY OF STONE AGE CULTURES DEAD IN INDIA?

Manoj KUMAR SINGH

Department of Anthropology, University of Delhi, Delhi-110007, India
E-mail: mksinghanthro@rediffmail.com

Abstract: The existence of Stone Age teaching and researches are going to be extinct from India in twenty first century. We have at least 40 Anthropology and Archaeology departments, where one can learn about Stone Age Cultures, but only one or two departments have specialist for this subject and near future, very soon they will be retire. Thus, the status of studies of Stone Age Cultures in India is really thinkable, because in younger generation nobody is working on this ever neglected field of research.
Key words: Stone Age, Cultures, Anthropology

Résumé: L'enseignement des galets aménagés et les recherches se sont éteints en Inde dans le 21ème siècle. Nous avons au moins 40 départements d'Anthropologie et d'Archéologie. Un seul département s'occupe de l'enseignement de la Culture des galets aménagés, mais les spécialistes pour ce sujet, bientôt à la retraite, existent seulement dans un ou deux départements. Ainsi, le statut des études des galets aménagés en Inde n'est vraiment pas pensable, parce que dans la jeune génération personne ne traite ce champ plus que jamais négligé de la recherche.
Mots clés: galets aménagés, les Cultures, l'Anthropologie

This is not a kind of research paper or report of new discovery or excavation's report, but this is my personal worried about Indian Prehistory. The first evidence of Stone Age culture has been found in India by Robert Bruce Foote as a Handaxe from Pallavaram near Madras in Tamilnadu state in 1863. After that around 50 years no body has done any kind of research work in India. The beginning of 20th century some foreigner scholars have done some work in eastern India and they got the evidence of Mesolithic and Neolithic period. In 1936 D. Terra and Paterson came to India under the banner of Yale Cambridge expedition and they tried to give a chronology for Indian Prehistory and studied in Shivalik deposition and compare the Sohan terraces with Himalayan glaciations, and gave first time chronology for Indian Prehistory which was the beginning phase of Indian Prehistory.

The big changes in Stone Age studies came when Late H. D. Sankalia joined the Deccan College and it was really a golden phase of Indian Prehistory. He has tried to get over all picture of whole India about Lower, Middle and Upper Palaeolithic, Mesolithic, Neolithic, Chalcolithic and Iron Age and gave the Ph.d topic to his students who were spread all over in India and they did very good work and finally Late Sankalia was able to published a famous book *"Prehistory and Protohistory of India and Pakistan"* in 1974. Same time the research was going on in the leadership of late G.R. Sharma in Department of Ancient History and Archaeology, Allahabad, they did very good work in Utter Pradesh, late D. Sen and Ashok Ghosh, Department of Anthropology, Calcutta University, they also did a very good work in Eastern India, and Thimma Reddy and M.L.K. Murthy they did a good work in Southern India. The contribution of H.D. Sankalia in Indian Prehistory will never forget. After his death V.N. Misra and K.Paddayya took the leadership and done excellent research in Prehistory in last century.

The beginning of 21st century was a downfall in teaching and research in Indian Prehistory, and last person who has done an exceptionally well in teaching as well as research was D.K. Bhattacharya, Department of Anthropology University of Delhi, Jacob Jayaraj, Department of Anthropology, S.V. University Tirupati and has retired in 2004, 2007 subsequently and very soon K. Paddayya, Department of Archaeology, Deccan College, Pune, Ranjana ray, Department of Anthropology, Calcutta University, Calcutta and Vidula jayaswal, Department of Ancient History and Archaeology, BHU, Varanasi, will be retire.

I belong to Anthropology department and at least there are more than 30 Anthropology departments in India, but except Calcutta and Andhra University Prehistory taught by either social anthropologist or physical Anthropologist, though the Prehistory is integrated and one of the main branches of Anthropology. It is big worried for Anthropology Department in India, and we should take immediate step to save and teaching and research.

I can draw the conclusion of my 10 year experience that students are not interested in this highly specialized field, and they opted either social or physical Anthropology where at least they can get a job in NGO or private sector, but in Prehistory one can only get a job either in University level or Archaeological Survey on India, where prospect are very rare.

Now there is a big challenge is how to save the teaching. We have to mobilized to the students and encourage them to take interest in Prehistory and further do research and try to create new job for the students, otherwise very soon teaching will be finish in about 95% Anthropology Department in India.

To conclude I can say 21st century need a very big revolution and good leadership in Indian Prehistory who can take care of Anthropology as well as Archaeology departments of India.

References

BHATTACHARYA, D.K. (2004) Prehistory of India Revisited. *The Eastern Anthropologist* 57:1, p. 29-44.

FOOTE, R.B. (1866) on the occurrence of stone implements in lateritic formations in various parts of the Madras and North Arcot districts. *Madras Journal of Literature and Science,* 3rd. series: II, P. 1-35.

MISRA, V.N. (1975-1976) The Acheulian Industry of Rock Shelter IIIF-23 at Bhimbhetka, Central India: A Preliminary Study. *Puratattva* 8, p. 13-36.

PADDAYYA, K. (1977a) An Acheulian Occupation Site at Hunsgi, Peninsular India: A Summary of the Result of Two Seasons of Excavation (1975-76). *World Archaeology* 8:3, p. 344-355.

SANKALIA, H.D. (1974) *Prehistory and Protohistory of India and Pakistan.* Pune: Deccan College.

www.ingramcontent.com/pod-product-compliance
Lightning Source LLC
Chambersburg PA
CBHW061304270326
41932CB00029B/3471